The High Society Bible by Ellora Spencer-Brown. Published by Glowpotion Publishing UK, London.

www.glowpotion.co.uk

© 2021 Ellora Spencer-Brown.

All rights reserved. No portion of this book may be reproduced in any form without permission from the publisher, except as permitted by U.K/U.S. copyright law.

Images reproduced with kind permission from pixabay.com and designyourownperfume.co.uk

We hope you enjoy this etiquette guide and find it useful. Please note that the advice herein is particularly suitable for British or other western societies. In some countries accepted etiquette may vary so it's always worth doing a little research before you travel.

If you enjoyed this book then as a small business we'd really appreciate a review on Amazon. Thank you!

Welcome to the High Society Bible

Dear fabulous, aspirational lady!

If you want to be the very best that you can be and earn the money and the respect that you deserve then you need to learn to thrive in the higher circles of power where affluence and great connections are to be found.

Your individuality ultimately holds the key to your success. However to get to the point where you're able to unfold your wings and shine gloriously down upon an admiring and appreciative audience takes a certain amount of initial conformity. You need to compromise *just* enough, fit in *just* enough, so that you can earn the opportunity to get your very stylish foot firmly in the Society Door.

You may find that some of this advice annoys you. You may find it condescending. You may feel that some of it is not particularly politically correct, and I'd be the first to agree. The higher echelons of Society are certainly still old fashioned, possibly even faintly ridiculous. But I present to you the Rules as they stand; those traditional, anachronistic guidelines of common decency and good manners, for you to pick and choose from as you will.

I strongly believe that good etiquette still has a place in 2021. Indeed I'm confident that an ever evolving theory of manners will reach out through time as Empires rise and fall. For at its heart lies simply the awareness of how to live sensitively and kindly with others, and how to bring the best out of yourself.

In life and in business, at any level, a knowledge of accepted etiquette will carry you far. It enables you to charm and influence others to get ahead, or it can simply give you an understanding of the manners and expectations of certain members of the elite so that you can seamlessly dwell amongst them where necessary.

Think of this e-book as your super quick, cost effective finishing school! Practise the things which you have learnt until the artifice segues into reality and you develop beautiful manners which come naturally to you wherever the occasion demands them...

...And then get out there and conquer Society! Or the world! Or whatever floats your private yacht ...

Yours sincerely,

Ellora Spencer

(Etiquette Consultant, Glowpotion UK)

CONTENTS:
Graceful Manners

- The Fundamentals
- Elegant Deportment
- Sitting Pretty
- The Art of Queuing
- Navigating Doors
- Graceful Body Language
- Uncouth Behaviours

Public Image and your Personal Brand

- The Secret of Style
- Wardrobe Fundamentals
- Make-up Mastery
- Scent
- Perfect Hair
- Lingerie
- Footwear
- Essential Accessories
- Tattoos and Piercings
- Classic Dress Codes

Impeccable Table Manners

- At the Table
- Settings and Protocol
- Dining Delicately

The Art of Socialising

- Public Presence
- Charming Introductions
- Making Conversation

- The Golden Rules of Friendship
- Cardinal Conversational Sins
- Verbal Giveaways

Everyday Elegance

- Finances with Finesse
- Handling Money
- The Art of Giving and Receiving
- Being a Gracious Guest
- Smart Smoking
- Inoffensive Inebriation
- Conflict Management
- Dating Dilemmas

Society Occasions, Events, Travel

- Restaurant Courtesies
- Hotel Courtesies
- The VIP Club
- The Opera or Theatre
- Beachside
- Polo Season
- The Private Yacht
- The Private Jet
- How to meet Royalty
- How to meet Celebrities

Entertaining and Hospitality

- The Brilliant Hostess
- Cocktail Party
- Scintillating Dinner Parties
- Throwing a Luxury Picnic

Charming Correspondence

- The Ladies Bureau
- Letters, cards, and Invitations

Graceful Manners

The fundamentals

The basics of fine manners depends upon a simple premise. That is, **to make others feel at ease in your company, and to be pleasant, considerate and honourable- whilst still maintaining an aura of individuality and a backbone of assertiveness where it counts.**

Good manners are a fine line to tread. It's all too easy to commit faux pas, especially in todays "woke" world, with its many avenues of potential offence online and offline- and as never before, it is often hard to escape past mistakes. One ill-judged word may simmer in the dredges of social media seemingly forever. One drunken mistake could be photographed and shared. So the benefits of learning to successfully navigate the path of good manners are beneficial for both your social and professional reputation.

What are the most basic rules of good manners?

- **Endeavour to be pleasant, considerate, and honourable in every situation- and in that order of priority.** You may find, in the case of an argument for instance, that you are disinclined to be pleasant, but try to remain considerate, or at the very least honourable. It may feel great to hurl insults or pull others up in public, but unless this is an issue of great societal importance, the moral high ground of a dignified silence or exit is a much classier place to stand.

- **Extend your good manners to all you encounter, however low down on the social scale they may appear.** It is the demonstration of kindness and compassion to those on the margins of society that really shows the true depths of a person's good breeding. All too often I have seen people, usually "new" money, who are all politeness to those they wish to impress with their wealth, but will dismiss those they deem beneath them with barely a second glance. This cheapens them, and shows the inauthenticity of their manners, which are not a way of life, only an affectation on the surface for show. A person who is truly at ease with their wealth is usually deeply aware of their privilege and would never abuse their position by denigrating others less fortunate.

- **Good manners should be genuine where possible, but you may have to fake it until you make it.** In essence manners are a way of making life more pleasant, by easing social interactions and providing a formula to ensure day to day society is conducted in a fair and stress free way. Most of us, if we're honest, have selfish and childish tendencies. The point of good manners is to keep these hidden, to bring to the surface instead our best qualities, and to encourage and enable others to do the same.

To some extent, good manners are a make believe. They are a social construct, but they are not quite a lie. They're simply a conscious decision to bring our best selves out in public, and leave the greyer parts of our personality at home. Don't think of good manners as being disingenuous or inauthentic, think of them as you making a conscious decision to be your best self every day.

- **Remember names.** This is such a little thing, but it is so important, and will mark you out as particularly considerate. People appreciate it when you remember their names or small details about them, especially if your initial meeting with them has been a brief one.

- **Smile and maintain a sense of humour.** Many an awkward situation or meeting has been leavened with a ready smile or some small attempt at a joke. If you or somebody else makes a social slip up or faux pas, this is your first defence. To make more of a mistake by being embarrassed or angry by it lends the situation more gravitas than it deserves, and will only serve to highlight your discomfort of the polite society you are in. Simply smile or laugh, shrug it off, and move on. Everyone makes mistakes. Even royalty...

- **Respect age, rank, and wisdom.** We are fortunate to live in an increasingly egalitarian society. However with good manners, certain rules still apply. Respect demands that we treat some people more equally than others, regardless of whether we like or agree with them personally. These people include the elderly or those senior to us, professional superiors, and high ranking individuals.

Remember, these rules are not made to patronise or disadvantage anyone, and were created with the very best of intentions, so try to abide by them even though they may appear old fashioned at times. They are simply a way of showing respect. Remember that each new generation tends to become more liberal than the generation before it- so behaviours that are considered perfectly normal amongst your peers may well shock an older audience. It is hard to change lifelong habits so have the courtesy to meet others on their side of the generational divide.

- **Honour your personality.** Manners are fine things, but remember they should be prescriptive. There is a lot of room for individuality and unique opinions. This means that although good manners should be generally and widely applied, they are also situation specific. Some of the most charismatic, beloved, and interesting people in society will exhibit irreverence and outrageousness where appropriate amongst their friends. The trick here is in reading the room, which is a learned with practise behaviour rather than a teachable one. Consider your audience and behave accordingly. That slightly risqué joke that had your friends in stitches could bomb badly in a more formal situation, for example.

Elegant Deportment

Standing Statuesquely

Standing straight with your shoulders back will instantly impress

Good posture has the power to instantly impress. It's a power that's free to everyone, although rarely taken advantage of- lending an advantageous element of surprise when it *is* demonstrated well. Whether you're clad in a ball gown with diamonds around your neck or slumming it in a riding jacket and your oldest jeans, good posture will elevate your look. It will lend you a certain presence and confidence. It will make the most of your height, and is more slimming than slouching- as weight is distributed more evenly across your body.

   To practise good posture you could resort to that age old trick of walking across the room balancing a book on your head. Try it. You will discover that to keep the book firmly in place you must hold your head high, with a straight back, stomach tucked in and hips slightly forward. When you have dispensed with the book, once out in public, it might help to imagine an invisible cord pulling you up from the top of your head.

   Remember, people with wealth and power don't scuttle about apologetically, hunched over like goblins, they walk tall and straight, with an assured spring in their step. Work on your posture to ensure maximum impact when you enter a room.

Sitting Pretty

No 1 Rule: Knees together at all times!

Sitting is a concept which although stunningly simple in theory is more fraught with difficulties on application. The act of sitting by nature denotes a period of inactivity or rest, so when seated in public try to be considerate of others by keeping jiggling feet or swinging legs to a minimum. Constant fidgeting is highly disconcerting. Legs should ideally be lightly crossed at the ankle, knees together, leaning slightly to the side. The Duchess stance. At the very least, **keep your knees together**- particularly when in short skirts or when entering and exiting cars or taxis. In public, if you are at liberty to do so, be ready to offer your seat to those who may need it more, the elderly, infirm, or pregnant.

There is absolutely no situation ever where it is okay to put shoes upon furniture you are sitting on anywhere but in your own home. Well, short of an actual threat to life perhaps. Socked or stocking- clad feet may be permissible in the company of close friends in private.

The Art of Queuing

Queuing is a subtle Art, with unspoken rules and terms of engagement. Never stand too close to others, particularly if you're queueing at a cashpoint. It's never acceptable to queue jump, even if your friends are there and calling you forward. Similarly it's bad form to save places for others. You may jump the queue simply to accompany your friends make a purchase, but you do run the risk of seeming a queue jumper and attracting censure.

When others jump queues it's tempting to confront them, but it's more dignified and ladylike to remain silent. You can be assured that the quiet wrath of the entire queue is now upon them, their dignity lies bleeding, and the moral high ground is yours. A slight frown is more than enough. If you're really lucky, someone with less dignity than you may even give them an ear full anyway.

If you have the time and liberty to do so, it's polite to surrender your place in the queue to the elderly, infirm, or pregnant, particularly at public toilets. You may choose to afford this small courtesy to parents with very small children too. This is a judgement call, as in some places you would be queueing all day if you let every senior person or parent and toddler in front of you...

It must be said that unfortunately not every country has a queuing culture. I will name no names, but in some situations you may have to be prepared to lead by example. In extreme cases you may even have to lower yourselves to their level or you'll *never* get served. This is sad, but again, console yourself that the moral high ground is yours. Be glad that you live in a civilised country with a queueing culture, and try not to elbow anybody else *too* hard.

Navigating Doors

Doors should be simple, but they can be a minefield. It's polite to open doors for others, male or female, if you enter in front of them. However, avoid holding the door open if they are more than a few paces behind you, or they will find themselves in that classic "trotting to catch up" situation, which inconveniences rather than helps them.

There are still gentlemen around who will go out of their way to open a door or stand for a lady, or even take her coat. Whatever your views, it's best to accept the gesture pleasantly in the kindly spirit in which it was meant. No normal man opens doors to women to patronise them intentionally, and indeed an older gentleman may be positively baffled if he is rudely rebuffed. Times change, attitudes change, manners evolve, but the meaning behind them remains the same. Respect the generational differences of old fashioned manners, and remember your all important smile and sense of humour.

Graceful Body Language

The expression you wear is even more important than your outfit.

Body language makes up over 50% of all communication. This means that if you can master it, you're already halfway there. Your posture, your arm movements, and your facial expressions govern your body language, and these subtle movements and behaviours have the power to either betray you or greatly assist you in society. So it's worth a few moments study and a modicum of conscious on the spot attention.

How *do* others see you in public? Do you come across as welcoming and engaging? Over excitable? Awkward, fidgety? Cold, intimidating? Often people are very unaware of how they are presenting themselves. Sometimes shyness can be mistaken for arrogance or disinterest.

To make a good impression on those around you and encourage them to engage with you, practise open body language. Lean towards them ever so slightly in conversation, and nod and smile appropriately. Maintain a good level of eye contact. When people truly enjoy a real connection you will often notice "mirroring" taking place in the conversation, which is when the two people subconsciously use the same body language. Hopefully if you're really being attentive and they are interesting this will happen naturally, but it's easy enough to fake if you need to, albeit a little contrived.

Avoid behaviours which give off an air of disinterest or boredom. Behaviours which give this impression include leaning away, folding your arms, fidgeting, frowning, or hunching over.

Facial expressions hold perhaps the most important body language cues. A gracious smile is a wonderful social lubricant. Use it again and again, but do make sure that it's a genuine smile and not a forced grimace.

If facial expressions are at the top of the body language hierarchy then the eyes are the crown. You really can tell a lot about another person by their eyes. Use yours to maintain friendly eye contact- which should long be enough to let them know that you're interested in the conversation- and even longer if you're interested in them *romantically*. Never stare off into the distance as if you wish you were elsewhere, even if you do...

Staring is rude. Especially if it is at a fault in another person, such as a spot or a bald patch. Prolonged staring can come across as aggressive and confrontational.

If you want to look at someone else during a conversations with a friend, do it surreptitiously by waiting a second and then casting a long panoramic sweep of the room with your eyes. Never point and whisper, or others will assume that you're gossiping maliciously about them even if this isn't the case. Remember, even if your lips are silent, the rest of your body is still speaking to the room. Hold it in thrall not contempt.

Uncouth Behaviours

Probably best not to dance naked on tables...

There are some unladylike behaviours which should never, ever be indulged in in public.

These are:

The application of, or checking of make-up. This comes across first and foremost as very tacky. Make-up should be a delicious secret weapon in a woman's arsenal. Secondly it comes across as somewhat unhygienic, and lastly, vain or self absorbed. Save the make up reapplications for trips to the bathroom.

Space invading. It's respectful to allow others space. Around 45cm is a good rough guide. This rule must by necessity be run over roughshod in bars or at other more intimate times, but should be adhered to at work or when amongst strangers. Remember to invade someone's personal space will either be seen as a threat or a come on, depending on the dynamic. So mind the gap, and keep the peace.

Staring. Excessive eye contact, particularly in close quarters such as in a lift or on a train induces anxiety in strangers. It's sometimes hard to know where to look- so try focussing on a point in the distance, to the left or right of the other person.

Loud phone conversations. Indeed, in some instances, such as in the quiet carriage of a train, any phone conversations at all. Never assume anyone else but you is interested in your conversation. If you must answer the phone in company, moderate your voice, and save any salacious gossip for a more private arena.

Phones, in general, should be kept in your bag over dinner or in company, and only surreptitiously referred to- perhaps in a conversational lull, whilst taking a picture, or during a bathroom break. It's obnoxious to eat your meal with your phone on the dinner table or to ignore your present companion for social media or a distant friend. The only exception is when a genuine emergency could be a real possibility, perhaps if you have caring responsibilities, for example, or are on call.

Unsavoury personal habits. If you've got as far as reading this then it probably doesn't need to be said, but in the spirit of due diligence: cover your sneezes in public. Wear a face mask if you're ill or when legally required to do so. Do not pick at noses, ears or spots. Do not suck your hair, bite your nails, spit, habitually chew gum, or wipe your nose on your sleeve *(unless utterly desperate)*. Carry tissues with you, and dispose of said tissues at the earliest opportunity. Where no bin is available, used tissues should be returned discretely to your handbag or pocket.

Inappropriate flirting or sexuality. There is a lot of power and fun to be had by revelling in femininity. Enjoy expressing your elegance, charm and womanly posture, but don't overdo it by seguing into fakery. Women who simper and overdo girlishness, twirling their hair and affecting weakness to attract men, might indeed attract the attention of the lower hanging male fruit, but their behaviour won't be popular with their friends or colleagues, and a loose reputation may ensue. There is a delicate line between friendliness and flirtiness, make sure you're on the right side of it.

Public Image and your Personal Brand

How you present yourself to others is important

The Secret of Style

There are far more important things in life than fashion, but nevertheless society judges on the outward appearance. So it's important to present yourself well whenever you're able to as the clothes you wear give others their impressions of you and do have strong social implications.

That being said, fashion is a fickle mistress. That which is coveted and worn right now will just as quickly be discarded for the next new thing in a week or two. This is fun if you're fortunate enough to have a healthy bank balance and enjoy near constant shopping, but rather disconcerting if you don't.

Whether you're wealthy, or whether you're not, it's advisable to ignore the vagaries of Fashion for the most part and aim instead to follow her less fickle friend, Style. Endeavouring to be stylish rather than merely a slave to fashion will ensure that there are always items in your wardrobe which will pass the test of time and can be pulled on at a moments notice. A capsule wardrobe of classics, as it were. A cashmere jumper or a woollen coat here, a plain satin slip there, a white tee shirt, a smart pair of navy good quality jeans, and so on. If you refrain from being a fast fashion addict you can spend your money on developing a core wardrobe that will serve you well for a long time. Shop strategically rather than impulsively if you're on a budget.

Love it or loathe it, fashion can empower you. High glamour might get you into that exclusive nightclub, power dressing can help your career, and dressing beautifully will always garner the attention of men, *(welcome or otherwise.)* So dressing for every occasion should be a conscious, deliberate choice. It will effect how others react to you.

Always remember that the world of fashion is fake. Photos are air brushed and taken with flattering lighting, often photo shopped. Models are unusually thin, unusually beautiful, and sadly a significant number of them have unhealthy relationships with food. Luxury labels are for the most part an illusion. It's fun to possess them, but many are made in the same factories overseas by the same low paid workers as numerous other cheaper brands. Far better to be discerning and look for real quality if your budget is limited. Real cashmere, real wool, real silk- will usually be better than something vastly overpriced in polyester with a fancy label on it. If you're able to afford it then clothing manufactured closer to home in the UK, Commonwealth, USA or Europe affords greatest prestige. In addition to the benefits of knowing it's been made by workers who've been paid a fair wage in decent conditions. Sustainable, home grown or ethical fashion represents the future.

Society will judge you whatever you do. Try hard to look good and others might label you a diva or assume you're on the look out for male attention. Neglect yourself and you'll be seen by some as "square" or slovenly. It's unfair, but you can't win them all, so don't try. Stay true to yourself. Just make sure that it's the smartest, best version of yourself that you're able to conjure up at any given moment- and if your tastes are a little risqué or out there, remember subtlety is always best. Never try too hard. It's always possible to inject a little personality into an otherwise stylish but unremarkable outfit. A quirky brooch or scarf here and there, a flamboyant piece of jewellery- there is no need to go in with all the guns blazing at once. Attention seeking, with the honourable exception of costume parties, is just not a good look on anyone.

Wardrobe Fundamentals

The Wardrobe Commandments

- **Manage your Assets**! Ensure that you never do big hair, dramatic makeup and heels, legs, or cleavage, all at once. This just emits an aura of desperation. Do establish what your own particular best assets are though, and don't be afraid to use them to your advantage. Just administer them sparingly for maximum effect. Gently tease. Don't get everything out all at once unless you're in the bedroom. Legs or cleavage, ladies. Never both.

- **Stock your wardrobe strategically, with clothes that fit well.** Have classics on standby for days when you haven't got time to plan outfits- Jean's and white Tee shirts, elegant but plain crisp cotton blouses and silk shirts, cashmere or wool jumpers, knee length tailored skirts and trousers...

    Don't fall into the trap of buying clothes that are too small for you "aspirationally". The truth is that no one will know what size it says on the label, and too tight clothes serve to emphasise rather than disguise your true dimensions. Cut the size tags off if it worries you.

- **Don't bother with waiting lists for luxury branded products.** By the time you actually get your hands on the piece a hundred lookalikes or fakes will have flooded the market. Far better to choose something equally as luxurious but far more original. Small or up and coming home grown labels show creative flair and are sometimes a good investment. Think about air miles and labour conditions too- is there a nationally renowned luxury label you could support closer to home? Genuine, perhaps bespoke, craftsmanship usually represents better value in the luxury market than mass produced replicas of the same item, no matter how desirable on social media.

- **Give thought to your colouring and the shades that suit you.** If you can afford it, get your colours done by a professional. At the very least get a second opinion in the changing room from an honest family member. Some colours will light you up and bring out the best in your complexion, others will have the opposite effect.

- **Use fashion tricks to look your best.** Block colours and vertical stripes are slimming, horizontal stripes and busy prints are not. V necks and open shirts will highlight your cleavage, as will a long necklace. Black is universally stylish and flattering. Three quarter length skirts or trousers will make you look shorter and stumpier. Never wear baggy clothing on both the top and the bottom or you will look dowdy and shapeless.

- **Be as pristine and neat as you can.** Make sure your clothes are at the very least clean, but ideally pressed and smelling beautifully of fabric conditioner. There should be no rips, deodorant stains, or bobbles in wool. Inexpensive small gadgets called lint removers can rejuvenate old jumpers.
- **Avoid clothes that are awkward and uncomfortable.** Tugging at or tweaking your clothes is never a good look. Make sure you're comfortable before you leave the house- practise dancing in the mirror if you have to. Remember, too tight clothes may rip at the seams.
- **Never show more than you mean to accidentally.** Be aware that anything that is a light colour or sheer is probably going to be see through in the light of day, even if it appears not to be in your dressing room. Get a second opinion before you leave the house. Thin dainty chiffon dresses and the like can be reinforced with petticoatery to give smoother lines and peace of mind. Muffin tops look very uncouth. To prevent them, go for a larger size or a higher waisted trouser. So called "whale tails" from visible thongs appearing above waistbands are truly horrifying.
- **Dress appropriately for your age.** There's never, ever anything wrong with dressing youthfully. A pair of jeans and a cute top can take years off an older lady- but booty shorts and their ilk may border on the bizarre and garner more stares than admiration. On the other size of the spectrum, twin sets, pearls, librarian hairstyles, and matching handbags on the young look just as out of place...

There are few hard and fast rules. Most items of clothing can be worn at any age. Just consider the effect of the whole outfit and adjust accordingly to tone it down if necessary. Keep the twin set and ditch the pearls, for instance, or rock the miniskirt but pair with thick tights and sensible boots.

Make-up Mastery

Make up is a wonderful tool which we can use to enhance our natural beauty and boost confidence. However it's by no means required, and indeed bad make up is perhaps worse than no make up at all.

The cardinal sin of make up is **wearing too much**. Too much make up, reminiscent of cosmetic counter ladies or air hostesses will always drag down the rest of your look, no matter how elegant it is otherwise.
  Make up is aging, and during the day you should aim to wear as little as you can confidently get away with! At work, aim for that "no make up" make up look. In practical terms this means BB cream, a flick of mascara, maybe under eye concealer, a muted or sheer and delicately shimmering eyeshadow. Perhaps the merest hint of blush, and a subtle sweep of lipstick or sheer gloss. Much more than this and it'll become obvious that you're wearing a lot of make up, and you will age and dry out your face- spoiling it for those occasions when you really want to pull out all the stops.

The golden rule for daytime make up is that you are aiming to present the **best possible natural version of yourself**. It should be lightly applied, with the result that many people, especially men, will fall for the lovely illusion that you are simply naturally beautiful.

Evening make up is a different matter entirely! When the sun goes down feel free to apply the high-voltage tools such as liquid eyeliner, bold lipsticks, vividly coloured eyeshadows and glitter. It's best not to employ all of these tools at the same time however, unless you're going to a fancy dress party or taking to the stage.

Never apply make up in public. This is incredibly tacky and comes across as a little bit vain. Make up should be more of a secret weapon, applied far from curious eyes. Far better to give others the impression that you woke up like this, because apart from anything else the application of make up is an ugly procedure. Who doesn't open their mouth gormlessly when they are applying mascara, for example?

Foundation is a cruel mistress, and should be tried out in daylight before purchase. When you choose a shade remember that you're aiming for invisibility on your face. There should be no visible tideline on the neck. Concealer to cover spots should be as believable as possible. Too much of it will end up drawing attention to the spot rather than concealing it. Pretty eyes and great hair are excellent diversionary tactics for bad skin or breakouts, infinitely preferable to caking yourself in unsightly cover-up. The contouring so beloved of Instagram models will fool no one in real life, so don't try.

Eyelashes should not be clumpy, and should be coated in waterproof mascara if there is any likelihood of rain. If you're making a feature of your eyes, go easy on the lips for subtle elegance. Less is more, if you want a classy look.

Brows should look your best version of natural. They should be plucked judiciously to prevent the hairy caterpillar effect, but don't get over enthusiastic as many people seem to or you'll only end up looking like some kind of surprised alien hybrid. Do remember that brows is a plural word. There should always be two of them. It's worth investing in a professional eyebrow pluck or wax, as the cliché that this can be an instant facelift is true.

Lipstick Is the cosmetic version of the high heel. It's quite high maintenance, and should be paid close attention to so as to avoid disaster. Avoid wearing very vibrant shades of lipstick in the office. If you have a bold shade on in the evening carry a small mirror in your handbag for impromptu checks. There should be no lipstick on teeth or smudges on wine glasses. If you have particularly dry, cracked lips then it's best to draw attention to another feature instead.

Nails should be clean, and no more than 3 mm long. Acrylic nails are sometimes necessary but shouldn't be the norm, as they *do* look fake, however expensive. The nails are always a good giveaway to show a high maintenance person, so never neglect them, as they *will* be noticed.

French manicures are a classy daytime look. Never have a French manicure on your toes though, likewise nail art or nail jewellery, as this just looks odd. Never neglect to check the state of your pedicure before wearing sandals or going barefoot.

Fake tan is the bane of elegance. Ideally it should be entirely avoided unless you can afford one that is so flawless as to look natural.

Public opinion is shifting and as we become more knowledgeable about anti ageing and health in general, it's likely that fake tanning will become less popular. Tan lines and stained clothing are just ugly. So too is an unnaturally, Oompa Loompa- like orange hue on an obviously normally pale person.

It's best to build a tan gradually and safely if you must have a real one. If you're interested in maintaining youthful skin for as long as possible however, you might want to embrace your natural colour, applying a high factor sunscreen, and leave the naturally tanned to rock their own awesome natural look.

Everyone is different and beautiful in their own way. Trying to fight against nature is always going to be more hassle and maintenance than aiming to enhance your own unique vibe. The same applies of course to any darker skinned ladies who are tempted by those dreadful whitening creams popular in some countries.

The Scent of a Lady

Cast an alluring aura with a carefully chosen scent

Perfume holds a potent power all of its own. Closely linked to memory, scent has the illusive ability to capture attention and announce your presence like a sweet calling card, leaving your memory to linger in the minds of your companions long after you've left.

The power of perfume, like all formidable tools, must be wielded carefully. The right amount is deliciously seductive. Too much and you'll give everyone a headache and attract attention for the wrong reasons. So, however tempted you are to shower yourself with your favourite fragrance before a night out, try to restrain yourself to one of two judicious squirts, perhaps one on the wrist, (high enough to not be washed off when you wash your hands after visiting the loo), and one on the décolletage or collarbone. The hair and the back of the neck are also alluring positions to receive perfume, particularly before a date.

If you wish to achieve a subtle but more complete coverage, it's effective to spray a cloud of fragrance into the air and then walk through it. Additionally, many ladies like to employ layering tactics to provide a longer lasting perfumed effect, so if you are able to buy a scented lotion to match your perfume then this can be helpful. Far better to layer, or even to reapply from a small decanter in your purse, than to leave the house knocking everyone back at fifty paces.

The element of surprise can be effective with perfume. You'll want to cultivate one of two regular "signature" scents, but try to mix it up a bit, and don't be a slave to just one particular label, go with your instincts here. Perfume should be intimate and it should tell your story, no one else's. The ultimate of luxury in perfume of course, following on from this, is a custom made, or bespoke scent made by a professional perfumer. You've truly arrived when you can afford one of these!

Tradition, and logic, dictates that lighter, fresher scents should be worn in the daytime, and heavier sultrier concoctions saved for sundown. The time of year also may effect your choice of scent, with fresher more delicate perfumes coming into their own wafting on a summer breeze, and darker, smokier, woodsy styles marrying well on a chunky knit scarf on a crisp winter morning. Wear what makes you feel good and you probably won't go wrong.

When you are shopping for perfume, be aware that there are different concentrations of perfume, and each has a different French name. Parfum is the most expensive, being at the highest concentration (meaning you need to use less of it). Eau de Parfum is the next highest concentration, and the most common. Then follows Eau de toilette and Eau de Cologne in that order.

Costly perfumes should be treated well and savoured. Do use them though, rather than just hoarding them for show, as they do have shelf lives. To prolong their quality, keep them away from light, heat, and never leave them unstoppered, lest they begin to denature before their time.

Remember perfume should be a natural and tasteful extension of a fresh clean body. No amount of perfume will truly cover up the woefully unwashed- so don't "French Shower" (unless you really are in desperate straits.) It really goes without saying, but perfume is no substitute for a wash.

Perfect Hair

Well kept hair can be a beautiful accessory, offering interesting possibilities for a fresh style to match each occasion. It needs to be carefully maintained however for optimal results, as unlike other accessories you can't just take it off easily and change it for another when you want a new look.

Salons should be havens of relaxation and quiet confidence in your stylist. Shop around and do your research to find one that you like and trust. Once found, a good stylist should be cultivated, so maintain hairdresser monogamy to increase your chances of a consistent quality cut.

Be aware that when you enter a new salon a good stylist will be looking at your clothes to ascertain your style, almost like the "cold reading" done by a psychic. So help them out, don't be misleading- save the fashion victim outfit for that trendy party and try to wear something that best represents your usual everyday beauty vibe.

Tipping is the done thing in salons, although many often neglect this in the UK, so there are low hanging social points to be won here. The suggested amount is 5 to ten percent of the cost of your cut/style in cash. Washers etc. should receive a few pounds of their own. The amount will depend on the expense of the cut and the quality of the establishment. In small town salons a few pounds is usually enough, but if you have shelled out a lot of money for the cut then it needs to be more, so judgement is needed here.

It's obvious, but if you're the fussy type, it helps to bring in magazine clippings showing the look or shade which you are hoping to achieve. Hair stylists are professionals, but they're not mind readers.

The best hair cuts to live with permanently are insouciantly stylish. In other words, they look great but are relatively easy to maintain. There's nothing wrong with trying out a complicated new style, but remember in life the lowest common denominator will out- there *will* be times when you simply don't have a moment to lose, and an easy style is your friend here. At the risk of offending some, know that very short cuts on ladies are not universally flattering, and indeed can be aging on all but the most forgiving of faces. Additionally, while we don't exist purely to please men of course, if you're looking to attract one, know that the vast majority of gentlemen love to see some lustrous locks on a lady.

The Top 13 Worst Crimes Against Hair:

1. **Greasiness.** Please regularly wash your hair. Even on rock stars not doing this still just looks..greasy. If you absolutely must go without a much needed wash for

whatever good reason, make use of a pretty hat or make sure you've got some dry shampoo on standby. Greasy hair is always less noticeable in a ponytail or braid.
2. **Head scratching and dandruff.** Heads can itch for all manner of reasons, and it's usually not because of poor hygiene, but do try to resist the urge to scratch. Innocent dermatitis or an insect bite could unfortunately be misconstrued for headlice. In addition, scratching will release dead skin flakes from your scalp and give the appearance of dandruff. If you naturally suffer from dandruff then know that this is a natural problem which many people suffer from, but do make sorting it out a priority if you want to look your best.
3. **Constant fiddling.** Fiddling and playing with hair can be a form of flirting, and sometimes girls do this subconsciously when they are attracted to someone or want their approval, or even just if they feel anxious in general. Overdoing it can make you appear overly girly or vacuous however, so if you think this is a problem you might have, or you wish to be taken more seriously at work, try to reign it in.
4. **Overuse of heated tools.** Try to save the straightening irons for special occasions, as overuse of heat will only lead to weak, damaged hair and frizz. On everyday occasions hair can be blow dried straight on a lower heat setting, or if you've got time, simply dried naturally with some serum applied.
5. **Bad dye jobs.** Aim for elegance and the natural coloured look. Never attempt to drastically alter the colour of your hair unless you know that you can afford the time and expense of regular upkeep. Visible roots are ugly and expose the illusion. Get advise from your hairdresser if you plan to go very light or very dark. It just doesn't suit everyone- you have to work within the limitations of your natural skin tone or you will end up

looking fake, tacky, or older than your years. Highlights can be very flattering, but should be subtle, not stripey, and within a few tones of your natural shade.
6. **Very ornate up dos unless at your own wedding or prom.** Otherwise you risk appearing somewhat fussy or vain, and of course at someone else event you would never want to be seen to upstage them.
7. **Androgynous haircuts coupled with tomboyish clothes can be misleading.** You must wear and be whatever you want in this world, and that's cool, but be aware of the message you are projecting if it isn't who you truly are.
8. **Tacky extensions and fake looking plaits.** Go hard or go home with these. Cheap ones will usually fool no one.
9. **Tight, high pony tails.** A low sleek pony tail or a loose bouncy high one can be very chic, but avoid extremely tight high ones. The "Croydon face lift" ponytail screams council estate unfortunately. *(Especially paired with hoop earrings, other exotic piercings, track suits, or tattoos.)* Most ladies faces benefit from a softer effect around the forehead, perhaps some soft wispy curls to give a pretty frame to the face.
10. **Extremely long hair.** Apart from being hard to effectively maintain, leading to knots and split ends, waist length hair looks very narcissistic. Get a trim, and enjoy the increased volume and healthiness of your hair. A certain amount of length is pretty, but make sure you are not in denial about its condition and volume at the ends.
11. **Aging disgracefully.** Everyone should absolutely enjoy looking as youthful as they can, for as long as they can. But this should be achieved with subtlety, elegance, and gradual graceful acceptance. Jet black, very dark brown, bright red, or excessively long thinning hair can look unflattering on a woman of a certain age.

Try to stick to a slightly lighter version of your natural hair colour as you mature. This will be softer, appear more voluminous, and more flattering. As will slightly shorter, perhaps shoulder length hair.
12. **Loose hair in speed boats or open top sports car.** Invest in a glamourous matching scarf- knots are never a good look and you'll damage your hair brushing them out.
13. **Dreadlocks.** Only ever appropriate if these are a part of your natural born hair culture. The rest of us will always look our best with the best version of our natural hair.

Lingerie

Underwear is oft neglected, being unseen by most, but it has an important role to play in the structuring of an elegant look. Carefully selected underwear can greatly enhance your posture and silhouette.

The golden rule of underwear for those who aspire towards elegance is that underwear should never be worn as outerwear- either in the form of exhibitionism or accidental slippage. Enjoy the role of wanton goddess in the boudoir, by all means, but maintain your air of mysterious allure by not giving too much away in public. Remember, the rarer the jewel, the more it is desired by discerning admirers...or in other words, a certain amount of carefully stage managed scarcity creates demand.

Bra Basics

The more nubile, modestly chested amongst us can get away with lacy, flimsy numbers, but the vast majority would benefit every time from a more structured bra. There are few things more inelegant and aging than a saggy bosom, so learn to embrace under wiring and supportive padding. In the long run this will improve the look of your breasts when you take off your bra as well, as they will tend to incline towards the position they remain in on a daily basis. With no support, bosoms succumb much more rapidly to gravity.

It's been said so many times before, but it's worth your while getting professionally measured. Many ladies are wandering around in the wrong bra size, blissfully ignorant of the unseemly skin ruching around their arms and back. As with any item of clothing, "aspirational" sizing will only ever serve to draw attention to your size in the worse possible way rather than complementing it.

When buying a bra it's wise to choose one that fits perfectly on its furthest catch extension- this way, over time as it naturally stretches, you can take it down a notch, avoiding bras that become too loose around the strap.

In an ideal world, underwear should match, especially if there is any chance of it being seen by a fortunate third party. In reality, this is often unrealistic. However, for fabulous first impressions with new loves, it's fun to possess a few beautiful matching lingerie sets. When buying these, its practical to buy duplicates of the bottoms if you can, as practically these become worn out so much quicker.

Try not to overexpose yourself. Avoid strap slippage, and make use of nude coloured underwear under light clothing. Test drive any strapless bra before an important event, as unfortunately some have a bad habit of slipping under the influence of even the smallest amount of sweat. Duct tape is useful in some situations- but always bring spare with you in your handbag so you're not caught out.

Be ruthless with bras, no matter how comfy! If they are faded, stretched and sagging, it's time to send them off to bra heaven and invest in a new one.

Elegant Briefs

Much that applies to bras can also be said about pants. Never buy them in too small a size, they'll create unsightly bulges, and always wear nude skin tone colours under anything sheer or white. Labels can be cut out to facilitate comfort and smooth lines, as scratching or plucking at underwear must be avoided at all costs.

For the love of all things elegant, please do not wear thongs out in society. The "whale tail", that embarrassing effect created when the top of the thong is visible above the waistband, is just so very lacking in class. By all means wear thongs in private, but bear in mind, few but the very slimmest and most toned can truly wear them to advantage. A pair of lacy French briefs are universally more flattering to the majority.

If you must wear thongs in public, stick to the hipster variety, or team them with high waisted trousers.

Hosiery

Tights, whilst certainly not the most glamourous of articles, are useful both for warmth and improving the look of your legs. A black shiny pair of tights will give the impression of longer, shapelier limbs, and a nude pair can even out your skin tone and prevent unsightly blotches in cold weather. Patterned tights can add interest to a look, but should be avoided if you have stumpy legs, as undue attention will be drawn to the area.

A general rule of hosiery is that the shorter the skirt you are wearing, the higher the denier of your tights should be. This rule can be happily ignored on very hot summer days, when maybe you might choose to not wear tights at all, but otherwise it will serve you well.

Choose nude coloured tights carefully. They should match your skin tone as closely as possible- being neither too pale, nor too tanned. Always bring a spare pair of tights in your handbag where it matters, in case of ladders.

If you're tempted to get adventurous with your hosiery, remember that fishnets are considered somewhat provocative (save them for fancy dress parties or Halloween). Tights in bright block colours such as red or green or blue may have the unfortunate effect of making you look like a gnome.

Stockings are the ultimate go to for hosiery adventures. Men love them and they feel seductive and exciting to wear. You do however, run a very real risk of having a strap ping off causing them to fall down, so they're best saved for sedentary romantic dates or intimate nights in.

Going commando will only ever be a risk, but of course, if you haven't done it at least once, you haven't lived...Just make sure that your outfit isn't see through and your skirt is gust proof...

Footwear

High Heels

It's rare to find a truly comfortable high heeled shoe, but for those heel affectionados amongst us, the benefits clearly outweigh the disadvantages. The right set of heels can complete an outfit beautifully, whilst giving extra height and the illusion of longer legs and tighter calves and thighs. They are impractical but fun, and if you walk in them correctly, with your hips forward and shoulders back, stepping ball to heel, there is a delicious feeling of grace to be felt as you sashay elegantly into the party.

Remember to be particularly conscious of your environment when you are wearing heels. Take off your shoes at the door if you are visiting other peoples houses, so as to avoid puncturing softer surfaces or tearing carpets. (Don't forget the advance pedicure here). Avoid sinking into damp, muddy grass, or deep gravel. Very pointed stilettos should be saved for events that are solely inside or in town.

Carry a small pair of ballet pumps with you in case of heel fatigue - sore feet can ruin your mood and put a damper on the evening- especially for your dance loving friends if they have to keep you company on the sidelines out of politeness.

Don't feel that your elegance depends on heels. They certainly help, in fact they're a fantastic addition to your glamorous goddess arsenal, but ladies who live in them constantly often develop unsightly bunions. For everyday wear, learn to love a more modest heel or cute Mary Jane's.

Selecting your footwear

Much like many other types of clothing, it is all too common to see people attempting to fit into the size that they would like to be, rather than the size that they actually are. This is unflattering with garments, and it simply won't work at all with shoes. The resulting blisters are ugly and painful, and the hobbling ludicrous. Don't think you can get away with too small sandals either, squashed red feet or heels sticking out over the sole are very inelegant.

At the other side of the spectrum, resist the temptation to pick up fabulous bargains from sales that are just a "little" bit too big. Don't lie to yourself, other people will notice. You will probably slip around inside them awkwardly as you walk, and in the worst case scenario, look like a clown. Remember shoes, especially leather ones, have a tendency to stretch and become slightly looser as you wear them in, so you never want to start off with a shoe that is too big.

When selecting a suitable and flattering shoe to match your clothes, do pay attention to the outfit and the overall impression you wish to convey. Certain combinations have become cliché, usually for good reason. For instance, you risk appearing vulgar if you team a mini skirt with towering stilettoes- save them for a slightly more modest skirt or trouser suit- perhaps choosing knee high boots, flats, or low heels instead.

There is a continuing trend of wearing sports or yoga wear as day wear. As someone who aspires towards elegance, it's best not to do this. There are plenty of other kinds of comfortable clothing that are infinitely more flattering and ladylike. You don't have to be uncomfortable or dressed up to the nines all of the time, but nor should you slog around in track suit bottoms or yoga pants when you are not actually doing sport. It looks unkempt, and the general impression brings with it a slight suspicion of sweat.

So no sports shoes unless you're actually at, or the way to, the track, gym, or great outdoors. Additionally, with the notable exceptions of tennis or volleyball, no trainers with skirts!

Polished to perfection

Shoes, even of the less treasured everyday variety, should be kept clean and polished. The toes of more expensive or delicate ones can be stuffed with paper to keep their shape.

It goes without saying that shoes should be as odourless as possible. Try to rotate the shoes that you wear regularly for long periods of time, to allow them to dry out and recover. Odour eating insoles, deodorant, and frequent changes of shoes can be employed if you suspect that your footwear is more fragrant than most. Remember, trainers without socks is asking for trouble even with the most innocent of feet.

Damp can also cause unsavoury mildewy wafts, particularly in trainers or hiking boots, so introduce them to the washing machine periodically, and if you go out in the rain, be sure to dry them out completely afterwards. All shoes have a shelf life, particularly ones you are very active in, so if you can afford it, be ruthless and know when to say goodbye.

Essential Accessories

To achieve the upper echelons of elegance tasteful accessories should be employed to add interest and cohesiveness to your look. The trick here is knowing when to stop, both in terms of quantity and "matchy matchy-ness ". Earrings and necklaces should match if possible, particularly with respect to heirloom pieces and higher brow occasions. It's no longer considered de rigueur to match all of the following however: shoes, handbags, gloves, hat, wallet- but some care should be taken to make sure that they at the very least look pleasing together.

If diamonds are financially out of your reach, don't be afraid to embrace tasteful costume jewellery. There are excellent laboratory made diamonds, Moissanite, or even simple cubic zirconia jewellery sets available- and by choosing simple, elegant pieces it is still possible to look expensive. Remember, most ordinary people, indeed even most wealthy people, are not diamond or gemstone experts. By projecting a glamorous image with all of the other aspects of your styling, combined with a confident easy manner around luxury, you will easily sell the illusion that the pretty stones around your neck could indeed be real diamonds.

Cheap metals should be avoided however, as a tell tale green staining or allergic, itchy rash around your neck looks very unsightly. If budget is an issue, stick to a good quality sterling silver. This will look great, but is within the realms of attainability for most budgets.

Sunglasses are beloved on social media, with labelled ones seen as highly luxurious and desirable items. However, unlike many, the truly elegant should not use them as an unnecessary means of flouting their wealth. Only wear sunglasses when they are actually needed, or risk looking nouveau rich and somewhat desperate for attention. Likewise, sunglasses should never be worn indoors, after dark, in the swimming pool, or when meeting people for the first time. Don't be put off though, as there is nothing more ageing than a furrowed brow caused by squinting at the sun. DO wear sunglasses, but only when they are genuinely required.

When it comes to watches, you could aspire to have several excellent quality ones. One for the daytime, one for the evening, and a lighter sports watch for outdoor pursuits. For the sake of simplicity and to be more forgiving on slimmer wallets, one, adaptable watch should be sufficient. Actually in the age of smartphones and their subsequent near constant availability in our handbags, many ladies are choosing to forgo watches altogether. They have moved from the realm of necessary tool, to pure accessory. So whilst it is desirable to possess a beautiful and classic watch, you may find a quality piece of jewellery to be a better, more versatile investment.

A generous bag selection should be cultivated. Think versatility here, they should come in various sizes and various neutral leathers (or good quality man made imitations). The aim is to not necessarily match your shoes, but be able to reach into your bag drawer and pull out a bag which tones well with each outfit. Allow yourself a few outrageously bejewelled, bijou creations as well, for special occasions where you want to stand out. You can't go wrong with gold or silver if you are aiming for maximum versatility. Remember, bags are accessories, but they also serve an important, and somewhat private function- never go rifling through another's bag without express permission.

Hats are underused in modern society, which creates opportunities for striking and refreshing looks if you choose to wear one. They are a simple but effective way of garnering attention. They are also flattering, and can enhance or soften your facial features. For instance, decorations or feathers can soften square faces, and brims can shorten horsey foreheads etc. The golden rule for hats is never to wear them inside except at weddings or very formal occasions, and choose one which suits you- neither too large nor too small for your body. In essence, wear the hat, don't let it wear YOU, and enjoy the air of charisma which this classic underused accessory will lend you.

Never underestimate the power of a good hat!

Another classic accessory which is not made use of as much as it could be is the glove. A fine, close fitted soft leather glove (or vegan imitation) is a wonderfully elegant thing, reminiscent of old school glamor, and will immediately mark you out as having exceptional taste.

Scarves provide excellent and versatile cover up opportunities, either to warm your shoulders over a dress or over swimwear to provide modesty as a sarong on a beach. If worn in the evening, they should ideally be fine silk.

Tattoos and piercings

I'm going to attract the disapproval of some for what I'm about to say, but this is an etiquette guide, so in the interests of full disclosure I'll plough ahead all the same. Tattoos and piercings (other than a single ear piercing on each side) are not universally chic.

Tattoos and piercings are many things to many people. They can be artistic, creative, sentimentally precious, meaningful, sexy, even beautiful, but the height of elegance they will probably never be...

If you already have a tattoo or unusual piercing, then, you do you! It's small minded to judge someone deeply on such a superficial thing anyway, and these kinds of people have no place in your personal life- but do know that you *will* be judged in some professional or societal quarters. Be aware of this in certain job interview situations, for example, and cover up accordingly.

If you're considering body modification, know that facial, neck, or hand tattoos, and septum, nose, or tongue type piercings are considered the tackiest. The so called "tramp stamp", or tattoo at the top of the posterior above the waistband, is quite frankly an unforgivable sin against elegance and should be covered up poste haste..(*I'm sorry, but its true)*. Belly button piercings can occasionally look chic, but only on the tautest, slenderest of abdomens.

You can remove a piercing if necessary, but don't fall for the myth that tattoos can easily be covered up. It's a long and tedious process and I've yet to meet someone who's tattoo has been rendered completely invisible- there's usually some discolouration of the skin remaining. Often its easier to have an ill judged tattoo transformed into a better one.

Tattoo in haste, repent at leisure. It's best to sit on any ideas for tattoo designs for a couple of months- remember you're going to have to live with it for a long time. It's an accessory you can never change or take off. You can actually get decent custom made temporary tattoos made up online- maybe trial your design first with no commitment before you buy.

Traditional Henna tattoos can be very pretty too for occasional wear, and also come without the lifelong commitment.

Interestingly, tattoos have become so ubiquitous among young people in the west that I'd argue it's actually more subversive and refreshing NOT to have one right now. Tattoos are currently in vogue, but like any other fashion, the danger is that they won't be in favour forever.

Classic Dress Codes

We live in relaxed times, which in many respects is a good thing. However there will still be occasions where tradition dictates, and the host eagerly anticipates, that guests will make an effort. Always do your best to follow the dress code on any invitation. It's only polite, and it shows that you value the invitee and respect the gravity of their occasion. Whether it is an intimate cocktail party or a grand white wedding, thought and time and money will have gone into the preparations. Your job is to show up and help to make the occasion sparkle.

If the occasion is somewhat nebulous, as it often is with more casual invitations, and no dress code has been mentioned- do your best to determine the correct attire. Of course if you know the host or hostess well then you can just ask them. Otherwise, consider the formality of the occasion, the cause of the occasion, the time of day, and its location. An early evening drinks invitation in a private home is likely to be less formal than a birthday dinner and dancing in a 5 star hotel, for instance. Weddings, anniversaries, christenings and funerals should be assumed to be formal affairs where you should make some effort (although in muted, sombre colours for a funeral, unless asked otherwise).

If you're unsure, it's always better to be slightly overdressed rather than underdressed. It's far more embarrassing to be the scruffiest, as it implies, truthfully or not, that you respect neither the host nor the occasion. It's easy to fix being slightly overdressed, as you can always remove items such as necklaces or dangling earrings, and it's always a good idea in principle to keep a smart but comfortable pair of black or brown leather flat shoes in the car, and perhaps even an emergency smart casual blazer.

If you're worried you're going to be underdressed, consider bringing a glamorous red lipstick, earrings and hair clips for an impromptu up do in your bag.

Formal daywear is the type of dress code you are most likely to come up against on regular occasions, such as relaxed weddings. Smart casual is even more relaxed, but ensure you are dressed smarter than you normally would be here- don't throw on any old thing. Trainers should not be worn, clothes should be neat and pressed, and if Jean's are risked, they should be of the non ripped, tailored variety.

In times gone by, people used to dress up for the theatre or ballet. Nowadays smart casual is often preferred, but consider the individual event. If it is a first night, if you have excellent seats or a box, or if you are being treated to a fine dinner then it would be appropriate to make more of an effort- with perhaps a cocktail dress and heels.

Remember, afternoon performances or events often carry on into the evening, so it may be wise to consider dressing a little smarter than you are originally inclined to, to take this into account.

It really goes without saying, but at weddings, never wear white (or even cream), and never try to upstage the bride. Dresses should be of the ladylike variety. A wedding is not really the place for ultra tight body con dresses and their ilk, especially if it takes place in a church or other place of worship. Think beautiful, not sexy- although with care, both can be achieved.

At long standing traditional events the dress code must be adhered to or you risk non admittance. At Ascot in the UK for instance, hats are non negotiable for ladies, and shoulders and midriffs must be covered. If trousers suits are risked, they must consist of full length trousers and separates must match. A similar traditional event, Henley, is more flexible about the showing of shoulders but insist that trousers are not worn and hemlines are no higher than one inch above your knee. At a very traditional event, it's worth doing your research first to make sure you will get past the doormen in your intended outfit.

There are two types of specific formal dress codes which may be mentioned on more prestigious invitations. These are; black tie and white tie.

Black Tie

Black tie is straightforward for men, as they are simply required to wear a suit, but much trickier to navigate for women. Hems of dresses should be no shorter than just above the knee. If your dress is on the shorter side, make sure that you wear stockings. Separates, such as a skirt and a coordinating smart top can be worn, but they are not ideal, although modern society has become increasingly more forgiving. Ditto trousers and trouser suits, which may be appropriate in more liberal company. If you do choose to break tradition and wear trousers, they should be very well tailored indeed. Avoid necklines that are deeply plunging- save them for the nightclub.

Tone down accessories when you are dressing to impress. It's always better to have one or two high quality accessories which work together well. Handbags should be as small and dainty as practical.

High heels are particularly appropriate at a black tie event, but make sure you are able to tolerate them all night, as bare feet are a no go. It's better to opt for the lower heel and remain in them throughout the evening. A warm wrap or silk cover up is useful.

White Tie

White tie is the most formal dress code, normally reserved only for balls, debutants, or extremely formal state occasions. They are rare, so consider yourself to have "arrived" if you are lucky enough to be invited to one. (Otherwise, why not throw your own? What lady doesnt deserve to be a princess for a night)?)

Dresses to follow a White Tie dress code must be long, with hems skimming ankles. Basically think full on ball gown. Cocktail or short dresses and trousers are not suitable here. You may even be refused entrance at more traditional events.

Décolletage, or the showing of cleavage, is allowed, within reason. Long gloves should be worn, but don't eat in them and don't wear rings over the top. Coordinate accessories, and wear your very best coordinating jewellery, bag, and shoes. This is the time to go all out.

Hair should not be entirely loose. A little hair may be down to fall flatteringly about your shoulders, but do take the time to style it. Up do's are very appropriate at a white tie event. A prior hair (and nail!) appointment would be welcome if budget allows.

Heels should be worn if possible, and they should be the best you can afford- although in a long ball gown they will be seldom seen, so do consider your comfort- you'll want to be able to remember this dazzling occasion for the rest of your life for all the right reasons!

Quality ball gowns, while heavenly, can be prohibitively expensive, and as they are rarely used it could be more practical to hire one for the occasion. Likewise statement jewellery.

Impeccable Table Manners

Table manners are one of the basic cardinal areas of etiquette, not least because the ritual of eating takes place several times a day, 365 days a year. It's important to enjoy your food though, and if there seems to be a lot to think about, remember that these rules are only to be strictly adhered to in company or when you are on show. Very close friends and family are *of course* expected to put up with the sight of you gnawing indecorously on a chicken wing or shovelling pretzels down your throat on the sofa.

Even in public though, the aim is to appear unstuffy, unpretentious, and above all natural. Your admiring public must believe that these manners come naturally to you. They are not learned behaviours, they precede organically from your genteel soul. Indeed most of these behaviours are pure common sense, and I'm sure I will be preaching to the converted, but let's begin.

At the Table

At the dinner table, sit up straight and don't fidget or yawn. Napkins should be unfolded and placed onto your lap. Be considerate, even if you're hungry. Think of others. Pass things, help serve, and don't grab. Try to take moderate portions, and come back for more if necessary. Ask politely to be passed food items rather than reaching across the table.

Sauces such as mustard should not be slathered over the food but rather placed delicately on the rim of the plate. To avoid offending your host or the chef, taste food before you cover it in seasonings.

Bring food up to your mouth rather than bending low over your plate like an animal at a trough. Try to pace your eating- don't scarf your food down at an unseemly rate nor pick at it all night and keep the others waiting for the next course. Take small mouthfuls, and it's so obvious, but don't slurp, or chew with your mouth open, or talk with food still in your mouth. Sneezes must be caught as gracefully as possible or at the very least, turn away from your dinner companions.

Contrary to some popular opinion, its perfectly okay to politely refuse food, but only if you absolutely loath it or are allergic to it or have chosen not to eat it on ethical grounds. It's far better to refuse something than to leave it sitting on your plate as though you just did not like your hosts version of it. Whenever possible though, do try a little.

Last but definitely not least, never play with your makeup or hair at the table as it appears vain and somewhat unhygienic too. Likewise resist the urge to play with your phone. It should be on silent and gracefully ignored at the table except for emergencies.

When to begin a meal is often a small minefield. It's best to take the lead from your host or hostess here if there is one. Once they have started it's perfectly okay for you to follow suit. Ideally, and traditionally, the party should wait until all of the guests have been served before they begin, particularly with cold meals. This is not always practical with hot food in busy restaurants though- often you'll be told to go ahead and tuck in, but it's graceful to put on some show of waiting unless told otherwise. A useful rule of thumb is to never be the very first to start!

While you wait, the bread basket is fair game- but don't launch yourself at it as if ravenous, even if you are.

Remember that dining in public or at a dinner party should only be 60% about the food- the other 40% is reserved for good conversation. So don't just turn up and eat. Attempt to make yourself convivial to add to the atmosphere of the party. This doesn't mean you have to be a titillating conversationalist, but it does involve listening to other people and showing interest in them, such as asking appropriate questions. If you are at a larger table, talk to those on both sides of you- don't ignore one for the other. Similarly try to have conversations that others can relate to and join in with; so no whispering or private jokes at the table, save them for afterwards.

There are some subjects which are best avoided in company, and especially at dinner, unless you are in very familiar company. These topics include the usual suspects such as anything of a disgusting or lurid nature, or anything possibly controversial such as politics or religions. Additionally, unless your dinner companions bring the subject up themselves it is indelicate to mention diets or the eating or drinking habits of others. Never ask someone why they are not drinking alcohol. Most likely they're just cutting down, but in the unlikely event that they're an alcoholic in recovery or pregnant and not ready to tell everyone just yet, it's best to pretend you haven't noticed.

It's perfectly acceptable to politely complain if there is something badly wrong with your food; such as a slug in the lettuce, or if meat such as chicken is dangerously undercooked, or if the food is incredibly over seasoned or hot food is cold. Try to be calm and pleasant though, unnecessary conflict is to be avoided, as it risks putting a damper on both the evening- and your host-who chose the restaurant. Never cause a scene simply because something isn't cooked to your own personal taste, but on the other hand, don't eat something that could be injurious to your health just to be kind.

If you spill something, request napkins or a cloth and try to mop it up. If it goes over someone's clothing, possessions, or fine tablecloth then offer up recompense. Most of the time it wont be required, but it's only polite to ask. On the other hand, if someone tips something on you, then as long as it was an accident, be graceful, refuse recompense, and try to laugh it off. Most likely the offender is feeling mortified, which is punishment enough.

Settings and Protocol

For the uninitiated it can be daunting to walk into a dining room and be faced with a traditionally set, formal table. In reality though, once you get over the sheer number of utensils, glasses and plates, it really is a very logical system.

The first and golden rule is one which you may have heard before- work from the outside in. Cutlery on the outside is intended to be used first, and as you proceed through the courses you will proceed through the cutlery. The soup course, if it is to appear in the menu, will likely be one of the first courses you are offered, and is to be eaten with the round spoon- the soup spoon.

If you find yourself in the position of setting a formal table yourself, remember the following: Forks go on the left, knives and spoons go on the right, and pudding utensils should either appear at the top of the place setting, or be bought to the table when required. Bread plates and bread knives, if present, are to be positioned at the left of each place setting.

Glasses will usually appear to the top right of your place setting. Don't be alarmed as in classier establishments there may be quite some array of them. You will often find a large, bowled glass for red wine, a slimmer wine glass for white wine, perhaps a glass for water or a tall slim champagne flute if you are lucky. A miniature stemmed flute or small tumbler indicates spirits or some kind or aperitif. You don't have to worry about selecting the correct glass, as in this kind of situation the drinks will usually be served to you by the wait staff.

If you haven't quite finished your pre dinner drink from the bar before the call to seat comes then you're allowed to take that drink to the table rather than waste it. Remember it's taking up space on an already busy table though, so dispatch with it as soon as practical.

When it comes to the actual manner and method of eating, take care that you are not holding your cutlery like a shovel. Instead, tuck the handle of each implement into your palm, and place your thumb along one side of the handle, with your index finger along the top. Never eat in gloves. Never lick knives, you risk a bleeding tongue, plus it looks animalistic. Never put the whole soup spoon in your mouth as they are normally rather large. Sip from the side of it instead, moving it gently away from you as you take each scoop to prevent spillage on your clothes. Likewise, to catch the dregs of any soup or sauce, tip the bowl slightly away from you to gather the delicious remnants, rather than towards you as many people do.

Napkins are there to protect beautiful clothes, so don't forget to use them. They should be gracefully unfolded and placed upon your lap (never tucked into your chin like a messy child). If you need to leave the table during the meal, leave your napkin neatly upon your chair to show that you are coming back again. At the end of the meal, leave the napkin upon or beside your plate. You don't have to fold it up neatly- if anything this will only confuse the wait staff who may mistake it for a fresh one.

If you find yourself at a particularly formal dinner, such as at a wedding, white tie or military or state occasion then you may encounter pre or after dinner speeches or toasts. Your job here is simply to listen quietly, tittering politely if jokes are offered, and raising your glass when a toast is called. At some of these type of occasions the National Anthem may be played, for which you will be required to stand. In Britain, if a "Loyal Toast" is called this is your cue to say " The Queen!" and raise your glass. These types of very formal dinners are rare however, in everyday life they are most often encountered in the military.

Particularly formal dinners in the UK may also include a ""Port Ceremony", where Port is passed around the table. The most important thing to remember here is that the Port is always passed to the left, clockwise around the table. It's considered unlucky to send it the wrong way!

If you are holding a dinner party of your own then be sure to use clean, proper linen napkins, rather than tacky tissue ones. (Although these are, of course, better than nothing). There are many pretty things you can do with napkins, folding them into intricate shapes and creating beautiful coloured themes for the table. The trend at the moment is for minimalism, so if you're all for an easy life, know that crisp white or neutral colours, and simple folded napkins are the height of good taste- and in fact, most likely always will be- as a relaxed, lived in luxury aesthetic rarely goes out of style.

When you have finished your meal, indicate you have done so to the host or waiting staff by placing your cutlery in a six o clock position on your plate, with the handles facing south.

Dining Delicately

Canapés or Amuse Bouche

Canapés, which are miniature finger foods, are adorable, but they can also be very tricksy indeed. In essence they are supposed to be small, bite sized morsels, which don't require cutlery, but can simply be picked up and popped into your mouth in one go. In the real world though, many chefs seem to delight in making them rather larger and more cumbersome than practical- so don't be afraid to finish your canapé in two bites rather than one if you need to. Just be decisive, don't nibble on it like a gerbil eating a pumpkin seed.

Canapés usually appear alongside alcoholic drinks, which is delightful of course, but do bear in mind the small, delicate nature of Canapés and try not to get tipsy too fast.

It's unbecoming to grab more than one Canapé at once, and you certainly shouldn't be seen to chase the serving staff around the room, so it's probably good practise not to arrive at a nebulous "drinks and nibbles" type event starving hungry.

You don't have to accept every Canapé you're offered, so feel free to politely decline ones you don't like the look of, or ones which look dangerously messy. Fish, such as king prawns in shells or smoked salmon often appear in the dangerously messy category- leaving the eater with smelly fingers or tail disposal issues. Don't turn them down if you enjoy them, but do head to the Ladies to freshen up, and dispose of shells as rapidly as possible.

Other risky canapés include olives, with stones to somehow delicately spit out, and cherry tomatoes, which can burst as you bite them and fly in your companions face. Proceed with caution. Never double dip a crudité, it's unhygienic.

Having learnt of the possible pitfalls of canapés, try to be thoughtful when planning your own event. Canapés should be small and dainty, contain as little waste materials such as shells or stones as possible, and messy or smelly foods should be carefully packaged to insure minimum mess. Dedicated plates should be available, and obvious, for debris. Take heed or you'll be discovering prawn tails in your flowerpots in the party aftermath...

Messy Articles

Vegetables

Artichokes are delicious but require some fine manoeuvring and expect to leave remains on your plate. Start by peeling off the plumper outer leaves with your fingers, scraping the goodness off with your teeth and then disposing of the remaining husk. There may be a sauce to dip the leaves in. When you are approaching the middle of the choke, you will notice some smaller leaves and a white hairy "beard". These are not to be eaten but to be discarded. The inner centre of the choke is where most of the eating is to be found, and a knife and fork should be used here.

Corn on the cob can be messy, particularly when lashing of melting butter are involved. Hopefully a cob fork will be provided to save your dignity. The most important thing to remember is that corn is notorious for sticking in teeth, so flee to the bathroom at the earliest opportunity for a quick check (and also to wash your buttery hands).

Peas are notorious for shooting off plates and into laps, and are commonly found squashed on the floor after a meal. To avoid this happening try to eat them in the correct manner, not by simply scooping them into your upturned fork, but by piercing individual peas on the prongs of your down turned fork. This takes time, but it prevents them rolling off to pastures new. Probably at home most of us, if we're honest, will resort to shovelling, but it's worth taking the time to do right when it matters.

Individual asparagus, such as in the form of canapés, should be eaten with your fingers, holding the stalk at the base and beginning with the tip. You can then discard the base if it is woody, as they sometimes are. Asparagus appearing in a main meal should just be eaten with a knife and fork in the usual way. Woody ends if present, can be abandoned at the edge of your plate.

The Cheeseboard

If you're helping yourself to a communal cheeseboard then it's important to be respectful and to go about it the right way. This improves the experience for everyone and insures the board doesn't look like a cheese tornado blew in and destroyed everything. Remember, quality cheese rounds, if gently and hygienically handled, can be reused by the host. Food wastage is never good.

So be thoughtful when cutting cheese. This will help everyone out and insure uniform slices. Round cheese must be sliced like a cake in triangles, triangular cheeses need to be cut lengthwise following the longest length, from the rind to the tip. Some cheeses, such as stilton, may be presented with a small silver spoon with which to scoop from the middle instead. However, its safest to only scoop a cheese from the middle if others have done so before you.

Don't be afraid to eat the rind of cheese, some consider it the best bit, although I wouldn't attempt this with a Babybel...

Meat

If you are presented with a large and unmanageable piece of meat, such as a whole game bird, never pick up the whole thing and gnaw on it. Try to dissect the limbs and eat each separately, then turn to the main body of the animal.

With meat, always try to use your cutlery where possible, assembling the meat into bite sized morsels. Some articles however, such as chicken wings, ribs, or lobster would be far too impractical to eat entirely with a knife and fork. Enjoy yourself, make use of the napkins provided, and have a good clean up in the Ladies afterwards. Order something else if you need to make a good impression.

Don't gnaw on bones in public unless absolutely necessary (such as in the case of the aforementioned chicken wings or ribs). Cracking bones and sucking on marrow, whilst rather intrepidly impressive, shouldn't be attempted in public. Lobsters of course, are the one exception to this rule.

Pasta, pizza, sandwiches, burgers

Lengthy pastas, such as linguine should be twirled around your fork, being careful not to flick sauce. If you're truly desperate its acceptable to slice the pasta up, but you will look very amateurish. Amateur is preferable to plastered in red sauce however. Whatever you do, don't slurp.

Pizza in a restaurant should be eaten with a knife and fork. At home, these rules should be ignored with joyful abandon.

Sandwiches must be eaten by hand, but traditionally they should be put back down on your plate between bites. Officially a burger is considered a sandwich, so knives and forks are not required here either.

Leftover parts

Delicately deposit stones, gristle or other objects in your cupped hand and then leave on the edge of your plate. Never reach into your mouth with your fingers.

Seafood

Bones and Shells

If you are going to eat whole fish on the bone then you have to do it right. This can be a tricky procedure for the uninitiated, so you may wish to order something else if you're in particularly exacting company.

To eat the fish you should start at the head and work your way down the spine from side to side, but never flip the fish over. Instead of flipping the fish over, you should gently lift up the spine with your fork and reach underneath. Even if you're a particularly adventurous eater normally, don't under any circumstances attempt to eat the tail or head. I imagine I'm preaching to the converted here, but there's always one...

   If you're eating a flat fish, there are going to be bones. This is just a fact of life. The trick is in trying to extract these bones in as undramatic way as possible, depositing them delicately on the side of your plate. Eating a flatfish is always going to be a bit of a palaver, so if appearances are everything and you want to make a good impression, it's advisable to order either a fillet of fish or an alternative dish entirely.

Prawns with their shells on present a completely different challenge. You're going to have to roll your sleeves up because this is a very hands-on experience. Begin by topping and tailing them, twisting off the head and then the tip of the tail with your fingers. Then peel off the shell starting at the head end and moving down towards where the tail once was. If there is an obvious black veiny string, remove this too. In better restaurants you should find a finger bowl has been

provided or at the very least a wipe of some kind. Do make sure to use it. Nothing is more off putting than fishy smelling fingers. Some restaurants may present their prawns already shelled with just their tails remaining. If this is the case, count your blessings, and pick the
prawns up by the tail to eat them. Always discard shells onto the corner of your plate, never into your napkin.

Moules et frites, otherwise known as mussels, should be eaten from the shell, but it's permissible to use a fork If you're squeamish. Use the bowl provided to dispose of the shells.

Oysters on Ice

Oysters, as well as being a supposed aphrodisiac, are a luxury, so you can be sure that they will present themselves if you're mixing in high society. It's fair to say though that as well as being a delicacy they're also very much an acquired taste. Everyone, with the exception of vegans or vegetarians and people with shellfish allergies, should try one at least once. But you're certainly not expected to do so more than once if you don't care for them. Indeed, there's no point ordering them in order to impress your company or your date, as lots of people even in the fanciest company never eat them by choice, and apart from anything else they'll be among the more expensive items on the menu. So if you love them, eat them to your hearts content, but never because you feel like you ought to, because when it comes to oysters, opinion can be divided.

How to eat oysters

Oysters will often appear on a sharing plate on ice adorned with lemon slices. The oyster should be lifted in its shell to your mouth and then gently dropped inside. You may need to give the oyster a small shake to detach it from its shell, or if necessary use the oyster fork provided, which will be found to the right of your plate. You should never chew on an oyster. Instead it should be held in the mouth for a few moments to savour and then swallowed. Most farmed oysters should be grit free, However if you do find grit or pieces of shell remove them as discreetly as possible onto the side of your plate.

Classic Caviar

Caviar is expensive and considered luxurious. It comes from the roe of the sturgeon fish, which is found in the Caspian sea. Caviar is normally eaten in small 30 g portions because caviar is a fatty as well as pricy delicacy, and a little goes a long way.

Caviar is eaten with a small serving spoon. You should take a small quantity of the caviar onto your plate. Don't put too much onto the spoon in one go as due to the rarity of caviar, and expense, it's understandably considered rude to waste it.

Caviar connoisseurs will often taste the caviar on the back of their hand, the part between the thumb and index finger. This could be considered pretentious amongst more casual company, but is a correct way of doing it.

Caviar can be served in many ways– perhaps with sour cream, blinis, herbs, salsa, or onions. Traditionalists however will always argue that it is best served simply, without accompaniment. The addition of some quality Russian vodka or champagne is always acceptable however.

If you find yourself in possession of a tin of fine caviar; remove the caviar from the tin and store it in a champagne flute if you have one. Store in the fridge, but let to come to room temperature before serving. You can tell if a caviar is good quality and fresh by the taste. A good caviar will not be too salty. If it is then it means that salt has been added to preserve it.

How to eat Sushi correctly

In the privacy of your own home amongst friends, feel free to bring out the knives, spoons, and forks. In public however, when eating Sushi or similar cuisine in a quality restaurant or abroad, it's polite to make an effort to honour the culture by doing it traditionally. Of course, it's rewarding too- so well worth taking the time to learn how.

First of all, learn to handle the chop sticks. This is best practised at home beforehand if you're over the age of 16, to prevent embarrassment and mess. To begin, hold the sticks together in one hand, with your fingers halfway down the length. Your middle finger should rest between the two chopsticks, and you fore finger and thumb should hold the uppermost one. Try to keep the bottom stick as motionless as you can, and use the uppermost one to pincer bite sized pieces of food.

Soy sauce should be poured out into the saucer provided. Offer to pour some for your companions if applicable at this point. The Wasabi, which is a hot green mustard made from a type of horseradish, should be mixed into your soy sauce with a chopstick if required. Sushi or sashimi should then be dipped into this soy sauce mixture. The top side of the sushi containing the fish or other topping should be the side to make contact with the sauce. Never just leave the sushi to soak in the soy or apply the condiments to the sushi directly- this will appear amateurish.

The pickled ginger, delicious though it undoubtedly is, is actually intended as a palate cleanser, not a pickle or garnish. So the correct way to eat it is between each different type of sushi.

Sushi should be eaten all at once, if possible, with the fish side down on your tongue for maximum flavour.

Miso soup is intended to be drunk straight from the bowl. It can be served as a starter or at anytime throughout the meal. The Japanese consider it a good hangover cure.

When you have finished, lay your chopsticks on your soy sauce saucer, parallel to the sushi bar, which will signify to the waitress you are ready for the bill. Hopefully she will attend to you promptly, but it's acceptable to summon her if she doesn't appear after a few moments.

Do

- Stick to Sushi in a Japanese restaurant if your chopstick skills are embarrassing. It's considered normal to use both chopsticks and fingers to eat sushi, so you can't get in too much of a predicament here.

- Order green tea, beer, or sake(strong rice wine)- it's traditional. Offer to refill others cups too when you help yourself to green tea or sake. These should be a communal activity.

- Offer the third piece of a sashimi set to your dinner companion. These come in threes, and are known as the "husband", "wife", and "mistress". To give the "mistress" to another is considered sweet and also good luck.

Don't

- Rub chopsticks together to remove splinters as this will be taken to insinuate that the chopsticks are poor quality.

- Point with chopsticks. It's considered rude, plus you might poke someone in the eye.

- Pass items around using chopsticks. Always proffer the plate.

- Leave chopsticks sticking out of bowls of rice. This is considered unlucky, as it is traditionally associated with funerals and leaving offerings for the dead.

- Order too much and then not eat it. The Japanese consider excess and the wasting of food to be very bad form; an opinion we could do worse than cultivate in the West.

Luxurious, Laborious Lobster

Lobster, whether you love or loathe it, is guaranteed to present itself at some point or another in high society. So it's a good idea to be prepared. Some restaurants will edit the lobster down, sending out just the claws and the tail, while other restaurants will serve it whole. If the lobster is whole, you could ask the kitchen to prepare it for you if you're desperately unsure, but this will highlight your inexperience to your dinner companions. Alternatively, another more subtle cop out for the squeamish is a dish called *Lobster Thermidor*, where the meat is extracted, mixed with a cream sauce, sprinkled with cheese and then grilled. This is delicious, and an excellent choice if you don't know what you're doing and are worried about making a mess.

How to gracefully tackle the lobster sitting on your plate:

1. The Lobster will most likely be served in the open shell. Begin with the easy to eat, ready cracked and exposed, tail meat, using a knife and fork.
2. Next, move on to the claws. These will probably come ready cracked too, but if not, make use of the special lobster crackers which will be supplied. These are similar to nut crackers. Crack the shell as gently as you can to avoid damaging the meat inside. Pluck out the meat as delicately as possible using the lobster fork.
3. You can eat the green tomalley (liver) of the lobster, and the pink coloured coral or roe if it is a female. You're not obliged to though, these are optional, and you are quite at leisure to leave them without incurring judgement.
4. If you're still hungry and you are in relaxed company, you can also twist off the legs, and as elegantly as possible, suck out the meat.

Lobster is actually a lot of fun, and to be honest pretty much everyone makes a bit of a mess eating it. Cracked pieces lay upon plates and forks will be worrying away and poking into small crevices for every last bit of meat. Lobster is very much a participatory experience, you can't really go wrong as long as you know what to expect.

Wine Appreciation

Wine can seem complicated, but it really need not be. Few of us, no matter how well bred, are truly wine connoisseurs. There is no need to fake it, or fake an interest If you do not have one. You will only be seen through very quickly by a real expert. However, there are some simple principles which will ensure easy navigation of the rarefied world of wine.

You often do you get what you pay for with wine, although there are always unexpected gems. So if you're no expert don't be afraid to summon the sommelier. Failing that, a safe approach is often to choose a wine in the mid price range, or in classier establishments a good tactic can be to order the house wine. This will be good value, but will have been carefully selected to reflect the quality of the establishment.

It used to be the case that finer wines tended to come with corks, and inferior wines with screw tops. Technology has meant that this is no longer the case though, so you are usually perfectly secure with a screw top wine. Do avoid plastic stoppers though as these do tend to appear in the cheapest, plonkiest supermarket offerings.

Purists often like to match their wine with their food. This is not regulation though, we live in modern times, and you're quite at liberty to drink what you want with whatever you like. However If you'd like to make some attempt at following the rules, it's helpful to remember that white wine normally accompanies lighter foods such as chicken or fish – and red wine accompanies richer foods such as steak. Rose wine is a great compromise if you don't enjoy either red or white wine, or if you're not sure which colour of wine would be most appropriate. To facilitate wine matching in a restaurant remember you can order by the glass.

Another traditional rule of wine is that dry wine is drunk before sweet wine, lighter wine is drunk before heavier wine, young wine is drunk before old wine, and lighter starting courses usually begin with white wine and end with red.

Nowadays the rules are considered very flexible, so don't worry, but it's useful to be aware of these traditions if you're confronted with a formally set table.

Wineglasses come in many different sizes and shapes. Red wine glasses are the largest, and are normally bowl shaped. White wine glasses are narrower, more like a tulip. Champagne flutes are the tallest and narrowest of all, and should be made of the best quality glass. Smaller glasses on stems usually indicate port or sherry, whilst whiskey and other spirits are served in tumblers. Ready mixed drinks can be served in any number of glasses, of course, so prepare to be surprised. Any glass with a stem should be held by the stem, to prevent unsightly fingerprints around the rim.

If you're in a restaurant in charge of ordering and are unsure how much wine to get, allocate half a bottle of wine per person.

If you're required to use a bottle opener to open a bottle of wine, make sure that you screw it all the way in to the cork before you begin to take it out. Sometimes the cork will break, if it does just laugh it off, and try again. Do make sure that you've fished out any broken pieces of cork before you serve though.

Wine Rituals

The Tasting

In a quality restaurant you may be presented the opened bottle for tasting. In the past this was to ensure that the wine was not "corked" ie tampered with or compromised in any way. Nowadays this is in most cases purely a formality, as many good wines will have a screw top. This is your chance to pour a small quantity of the wine, to have a dainty sniff and a sip.

You are tasting the wine to make sure that it is of good quality, so now is your chance to send it back if it smells vinegary or musty, or is sedimented, or has pieces of cork floating on it. This isn't really about your taste preferences at this stage however. Once the bottle is opened then assuming it is good then it would be rude to send it back simply because it does not taste quite how you imagined it would. If the wine is fine but you just don't like it then I'm afraid you're going to have to either endure it or order an additional one. Do request another from the waiter if the quality is poor though. The waiter is also on hand to make sure that the wine is chilled or bought to room temperature or decanted as required, so never be afraid to ask.

The Performance

In the higher echelons of the dining world refills may be administered by the waiter. In these cases be aware that your glass is likely to be filled rather briskly again upon emptying, so you may wish to take your time over your drink and leave a little remaining if you've had enough or wish to pace yourself.

In situations where you or your companions are responsible for refills, several rules apply. The first of these is that it is important to *look* as though you are drinking in moderation even if you aren't. To achieve this noble illusion glasses should ideally be filled only to the half full level each time- although you might get away with three quarters, but don't push your luck! The second rule of pouring is that top ups should be a communal activity, so don't be selfish, offer top ups to those around you every time you make a move to replenish your own glass.

When you're in very casual company with friends, remember to ignore these rules with glorious abandon!

Correct Temperatures

Temperature is an important consideration when it comes to wine, and getting it right can really enhance the flavour. Most red wines, with exception of Beaujolais, are at their best at room temperature. Decanting the wine into another vessel can ramp up the aesthetics and also allow the wine to breathe as it comes to temperature, so consider doing this if you have an elegant cut glass decanter or some such. Two hours at room temperature is an appropriate amount of time to leave a red wine to breathe.

White wines should always be served chilled, and never decanted. You can chill the wine in the fridge, but for maximum impact use an ice bucket.

Rose wines are a matter of personal preference- however when in doubt serve chilled.

The Champagne Lifestyle

When only the best will do, out comes the champagne! The opening of Champagne should be done with subtly and grace, a gentle sigh- no dramatic plumes of foam please, unless you're at the Grand Prix or launching a yacht. Remember, only those for whom Champagne is a rarity make a big deal out of it. If you wish to look to the manner born, you have to be discrete.

Never shake a champagne bottle. It's full of bubbles just waiting to escape. Point away from eyes and keep your thumb on the cork as you open it- a brave attempt to prevent it flying away (which may or may not be successful). Before opening, gather round your audience, champagne flutes in hand, ready to catch the bubbles and prevent wastage. Pour a little into each waiting flute, to make sure everyone gets some, and then go around topping up more fully. As with wine, flutes shouldn't be overfilled, and should be held by the stem. It is traditional to hold the champagne bottle as you pour by placing your thumb at the bottom of the bottle in the hollow and splaying your fingers across the base. This can be tricky though, especially if you have small hands. It would be far greater a faux pas to drop the bottle, so feel free to just grab it by the base. Don't be surprised if you see others, particularly older men, doing this though.

Champagne flutes should be tall, narrow, and made of clear glass to preserve the bubbles and showcase the hue. They should be scrupulously clean, as any detergent residue will kill the bubbles. Champagne bottles come in various sizes, with interesting names, depending on the size. A bottle containing two standard sized bottles of champagne is called a Magnum. A bottle containing four standard sized bottles is called a Jerobaum. Larger bottles than that actually exist too, called Rehobaums, Methuselahs, Balthazars and Nebuchadnezzars, containing 6, 8, 12, 16, and 20 bottles respectively. These are impractical though, and mainly appear for show on very ostentatious occasions.

Champagne deserves the best and so it really should be served in an ice bucket wherever possible.

Cocktails and Fine Spirits

Every girl worth her social "salt" who means to entertain should curate her own household drinks cabinet. This doesn't need to be excessive, we're not talking a full on minibar here, but it should contain the essentials which will enable her or her guests to knock up a selection of classic and crowd pleasing drinks, to suit most tastes. This household drinks cabinet could contain something like the following:

- Simple cocktail making equipment- think shaker, muddler, strainer.

- The glasses- whisky tumblers, Martini style glasses, highball glasses perhaps.
- The drinks- versatile classics such as gin, whisky, vodka, rum, Cointreau. Remember some spirits aficionados tend to be quite discerning, so it's worth investing in a smaller selection of quality bottles rather than a vaster array of cheap supermarket own brands.
- Other extras for making well known cocktails include: crushed ice, lemons or limes, Angostura Bitters, Creme de Cassis.
- Don't forget the mixers- orange juice, lemonade, ginger beer, tonic water, cranberry juice, iced tea, coke etc.

If this seems like a lot, don't worry as you don't need to keep all of it in stock, just pick a selection which you know to be popular in your own particular social orbit.

Some ladies are lured in by all sorts of pretty cocktail paraphernalia such as umbrellas, sparklers and suchlike. These are really quite lame and mostly seen on holiday resorts. True appreciators of spirits often feel that the quality of the drink should speak for itself, with few distractions, and accessories only added if they actually add something to the drink- such as a cherry, or a sliver of lime, or mint. Decorative cocktail stirrers or spherical ice cube moulds can be bought which bring the bling whilst still keeping everything stylish. If you absolutely must have umbrellas though, remember, your house, your rules!

Aperitifs:

Aperitifs are before dinner drinks which are intended to both stimulate the appetite and palate and help socially lubricate the beginnings of a good evening. Traditionally Aperitifs are light. They are intended to stimulate rather than overwhelm your taste buds. Suitable Aperitifs you could choose to drink before dinner include gin and tonic, Martini, Sherry or Vermouth. Any clear spirit mixture is a safe choice.

Digestifs:

Digestifs are after dinner drinks which although it's unlikely they actually do anything to improve your digestion, are still, traditionally in some circles indulged in after dinner. Think of them as nightcaps. These can be neat, and quite alcoholic, and are often darker spirits such as Armagnac, whisky, Cognac, or brandy.

Whisky:

Whisky is a matter of quite some gravity for a select few, so it's worth doing it right in case you find yourself up against such a person. Here are the ground rules:

1. Never chill whisky- the depths of flavour of quality whiskies are best appreciated at room temperature.
2. Serve in a glass tumbler with a thick bottom. If you can, serve whisky with a small jug of room temperature water (not sparkling).

Vodka:

Vodka should ideally be served very cold, so keep it in the fridge or pop it in the freezer for ten minutes beforehand.

Pastis, Absinthe, Ouzo

Like whisky, these should also be served with a small jug of room temperature water.

Swigging it straight

Never swig any drink, particularly spirits, from the bottle or you risk bringing homeless alcoholic vibes. Similarly, shots, whilst they are fun and do have a niche in life, are not elegant. If you crave a quick fix or a pure spirit, whisky is a much classier choice.

The Art of Socialising

Public Presence

To appear in public is to be on show. Like it or not, the world is your stage and you will be judged privately and professionally, and dealt with by others accordingly.

Maintain your poise at all times. Try to seem confident even if you aren't. Work hard to disguise feelings of boredom or exasperation, and save high emotions for the privacy of your own home. Try not to squawk or screech too loudly or over excitably with your girl friends- a lower, more moderated tone will lend an air of dignity.

Punctuality is important. There is no such thing as "fashionably late", there is only ever tardiness. Even with the luxury of mobile progress reports, lateness still isn't justified. Never, ever be late if you can help it for a business meeting or a one on one (where your companion waits for you all alone). Casual meetings at someone's home allow a little more leeway. In fact you should never turn up early for a dinner party in case they're not ready for you and are still in the kitchen. For 7 for 7.30's it's quite acceptable to be at the later end of the time frame, but never exceed 7.25 or you will keep everybody in suspense.

Of course, there will inevitably be times in life when you're running late. At times like these the most important thing to do is to let people know- and be realistic about your time scales- don't say 10 minutes when you mean half an hour. If some poor soul is waiting alone in a public place for you then you really do owe them a phone call. A text just doesn't cut it in this situation- you need to be sure that they have got the message and know you haven't forgotten all about them

Be conscientious and accountable. Try to arrive when you say you will, reply to texts, emails and phone calls, and never break your word. If you have to cancel a paid for event at the last minute, make sure you reimburse the money, and if you ever find yourself double booked you should always honour the first commitment (with the exceptions of important family or life events such as weddings). It's perfectly acceptable to apologise and decline an event because of a "prior engagement". Never fake sickness unless you're 100% sure you won't be discovered in your lie either on social media or in real life. If you're leaving one social engagement to head off to another one in the same evening, be very subtle about it or you risk offending your first host. If challenged, tell them you had already promised yourself to the first event but you simply couldn't miss calling in on this one for a little while because you wanted to see them so very much...

Always show gratitude when people render you small services in public. Be pleasant and as generous as you are able to with waiting staff, bell boys, and the like. Tipping is not expected in Britain as it is in America, as there is a national minimum wage although it is considered a bonus and usually appreciated. Be sure to do your research when going abroad so as to make sure you are not offending anyone or seen as mean. Some countries such as Japan consider tipping even a little rude, as it implies you think they are not earning enough..

Charming Introductions

First impressions are important and you can't take them back, so try to get it right the first time. It's customary to offer your hand to shake when you meet someone for the first time. This is often overlooked nowadays and you see two people standing facing each other awkwardly with their hands swinging down like a gorilla or even worse, in their pockets. When meeting someone for the first time, stand up, and offer your hand for a firm, but non aggressive handshake. State your name clearly-"Hello, nice to meet you. I'm Sarah."

Nice to meet you, or lovely to meet you, or great to meet you, are good platitudes to roll out upon meeting new people. Even just a simple, more casual "Hello, I'm Ella" is fine. "How do you do" is still used in some quarters but it is becoming less common and a little old fashioned. If someone does direct a "How do you do" at you, remember that although it sounds like a question it actually takes the place of a greeting, so reply with "how do you do", not "Thank you, I'm very well".

Some cultures are more touchy feely than you might be used to, so be prepared for surprise kisses on the cheek. If you'd rather avoid the kissing, pre-empt it by holding your hand out as quickly as possible. If all else fails though it's best to just accept your fate politely, as it would look like you were disgusted by them if you backed off in the opposite direction. This doesn't apply in situations where you ARE actually disgusted by them however, and if someone's being creepy or taking advantage then by all means get out of the situation. But oftentimes the gesture is kindly meant, just lost in cultural translation, and its polite to meet them half way by at least accepting the gesture, if not actively reciprocating yourself.

If you're the kisser not the kissee, make sure that you know the person well enough to make such a gesture. As a general rule, unless it's the done thing in your particular culture don't proffer kisses to people you don't know very well, they'll most likely feel alarmed. The same applies to hugs.

Introducing people and making it seem effortless is an art form in itself. Some hostesses will shirk this duty, operating from the premise that everyone will simply introduce themselves, but the reality is, many people are socially awkward or just a little shy and will breathe a huge sigh of relief if the host takes responsibility. It will just make the whole evening flow better.

Introduce other people to each other according to their status. This sounds complicated but it's really not- and by status we do not necessarily mean importance of course- but the traditional rules of courtly manners. Thus, ladies should be introduced to gentlemen, rather than the other way around. "Oliver, this is my friend Bella", and seniors should be introduced to younger people, "Bella, this is my granddad Harry". (Traditionally age trumps gender, so if the lady is younger, introduce the senior person to the lady.) If at a business rather than social meeting, then you should of course introduce according to rank in the company.

If you are introducing one person to a group, then introduce the individual to the group, rather than the group to the individual-" Charlotte, I'd like you to meet my work colleagues. Everyone, this is Charlotte". If you're introducing a couple to others then introduce them individually, they're not surgically attached, but it's helpful to outline their relationship to others. It seems cliché, but adding little details during introductions can help bolster the conversation. Try not to make it too contrived, but elaborate on your relationship with the person being introduced if you can. "Miranda is my yoga teacher" for example, or "James is a keen golfer too, So I'm sure you'll have plenty to talk about".

Forgetting acquaintances names is a cardinal sin, so do try to make a point to remember peoples names if you are ever likely to encounter them again. Try to style out your forgetfulness with maximum tact- by discretely asking someone else to remind you of their name before you talk to them. If you're caught on the spot then if plausible try to blame the noise levels at your last meeting, alternatively just avoid the subject altogether and do your research later. Jump straight into conversation with a leading question which will hopefully trigger your memory- "Hello! Lovely to see you again! What have you been up to lately?"

If you're on the opposite end of this scenario then try to have some mercy, even if you're a little offended. Remind them of your name, or the correct way of saying it, and offer up some sop to make them feel better- " don't worry it was so crazy/busy/hectic/noisy that night, I'm not surprised you've forgotten. At any business networking type events practise some future damage limitation by asking for a business card or details on the spot. You may think that you'll remember their name, but after the fifth introduction that evening, you probably won't.

Making Conversation

Disarm your audience with a winning smile!

You don't have to be hilarious or a great conversationalist to be charming company. Some people will naturally excel at making conversation and making other people feel at ease, but if you're not one of these people, don't worry. To a great extent conversation is a skill which can be studied, and if not mastered, at the very least greatly improved. So social lepers be encouraged, all is not lost.

There are several things you can do to give yourself a boost in the conversation stakes. First of all, try to keep up with current affairs and what is going on in the world. You don't have to have an in depth knowledge of the stock market or political situations in countries across the world, to be honest many people would find these topics dull anyway, but endeavour to cultivate a breadth of ideas by being as well read as you can. Check into the news every morning for fifteen minutes, or as you are getting ready for that party, just to spark a few interesting, topical gambits of conversation if you are stuck.

Another very easy way to be considered good company is simply to listen. Ask open ended questions, then wait for the reply (don't simply interview) and give one hundred percent of your attention to the person you are speaking with. By making your companion feel like the centre of your world, you'll endear yourself to them greatly- it's such a rare thing to be truly listened too. Even if you're bored in a conversation, don't visibility eye up your escape or more interesting people across the room. Manufacture a suitable excuse to speak to someone else subtly.

Don't be afraid of small talk. It has a monotonous and cliched reputation, but you have to start somewhere after all; and many people would like to have a conversation with you but just don't know how to start. A simple, possibly even dull, "How are you?" can sometimes take the asker to the most interesting places and deepen shallow acquaintances.

The true art of conversation lies in being a little surprising, even sometimes a tiny bit controversial. This is because most interesting conversations are quite personal, and take place outside of the bounds of small talk or mere pleasantries- but judge your audience. Don't ask intimate questions directly to people you don't know very well, but subtlety imply the question, giving them the chance to open up if they want to.

Help out the socially inept and shy, but never be so afraid of an awkward silence that you chatter on inanely and too fast and frighten them. It's better to have a slow and slightly stilted conversation than none at all however, so be kind enough to make the first move; and remember if someone is shy then drawing attention to it by pointing it out will only serve to make them feel one hundred times worse and the conversation even more awkward.

The true measure of a person is often how they treat their enemies. Be civil if you can, at all times and in all situations. Simply avoid certain others if necessary, and if you absolutely can't master your emotions in a particular persons presence then remember you're allowed to leave the situation. It's better to make a graceful dignified exit than a huge embarrassing scene- and you can always blame an urgent phone call or a headache for your departure if you'd prefer not to air your dirty linen to curious bystanders.

The Golden Rules of Friendship

1. Be reliable, be there for them even when they're sad and boring, and never make promises you can't keep.
2. Look out for your friends. Don't leave them all alone at parties and rescue them from unwanted advances and other awkward situations. Avoid being two faced, either have the courage to discuss your grievance with the guilty party, or say nothing. Remember most gossip has an inconvenient habit of being fully traceable to its source- a person who will gossip about another friend will have no qualms in exposing *you*.
3. Make important life events such as weddings, christenings, and birthdays a priority. Never bail on these unless it really is an emergency- and don't forget to bring an (in your personal budget) present and a card to all of these events.
4. Always extend the benefit of the doubt. If a friend is neglecting you, make sure it's not because they're depressed or suffering through some kind of

emergency before you freeze them out or send them that exasperated message.
5. Be as generous as you can with those you care about, and in return, reward *their* generosity. If someone does you a favour, thank them in kind- a card perhaps, or a little gift. This will make them feel appreciated rather than put upon, and keep them sweet for future favours when needed.
6. Try to keep envy at bay if your friend is more successful or better than you in some aspect of her life. Just be happy that someone so awesome is your friend- it will only reflect well on you. If you're the one who has the upper hand in some way, make sure you are tactful about it. Never suggest expensive bars or restaurants if you are wealthier, for instance, unless you are going to insist on paying for her.
7. Never flirt with your friends boyfriend or meet up with him without her (unless you're very old friends and have her blessing.) If your friend is flirting with *your* boyfriend then aim to meet up with them separately when you can to avoid an uncomfortable confrontation. Give her the benefit of the doubt if she's just a naturally friendly person as she probably just wants you all to get along. If she really has crossed the line though you will need to speak to her quietly, but directly. Make sure your boyfriend hasn't been encouraging it. Often girls are too quick to blame the "other" woman, as the reality that their boyfriend is a cad is not what they want to hear. Remember, most boyfriends will come and go, your best friends should be for life. But shameless and repeated boyfriend poaching is always a friendship deal breaker, so never stand for it.
8. Be as gentle as you can with platonic friends if you suspect they have a crush on you. If you don't feel the same way it's best to drop some subtle hints and let them know. Be kind, be complimentary (they're your

friend so they presumably have good qualities even if you're not attracted to them), but don't keep them on a string, forever hoping you'll throw them some crumbs of affection. For the most devotedly lovelorn of platonic friends, you may have to be more frank, and maybe even put a little distance between you. Let them move on emotionally. Never be one of these girls who keeps multiple men on the back burner because she loves basking in constant male attention. It's classier to be alone than leading somebody else on capriciously .

Cardinal Conversational Sins:

Forgetting names. This is the worst. Don't do this!

Arrogance, boasting, and showing off are a really bad look. In addition it comes across as somewhat "try hard" or desperate. Truly wealthy and well connected people don't have anything to prove, and other wealthy and well connected people know this.

Gratuitous foreign usage dropped into everyday conversation. Emphasis on "gratuitous". This is connected to the previous point, as it can come across as pretentious and somewhat "try hard". Its admirable that you're cosmopolitan and familiar with other languages but unless your companions have achieved a similar level of familiarity with the language then they're only going to be confused. This doesn't apply of course to speaking fully in a foreign language – just when words are used gratuitously, mainly to impress, amongst people who you know will have no idea what you're talking about.

Stubborn ignorance. It's great to have an opinion, and it's fun to have a debate; but try to develop the humility to recognise when you're out of your intellectual depth in a conversation. It will make you seem so much more intelligent if you're wise enough to admit when you know little about a particular subject, and are able to listen, ask questions and learn, rather than blindly wading in with ridiculously wrong ideas...As the saying goes, *"it's better to stay silent and feel like a fool, than to open your mouth and prove it".*

The Verbal Minefield – Class giveaways

You may or may not care whether you sound like an established member of high society or a nouveau rich, but if you do happen to care then there are a few words you should eschew so as to not blow your cover...

English words which mark you out as nouveau rich – and alternatives to choose instead:

Toilet. Choose lavatory or loo.

Mum and Dad. Probably too late to change this, but wealthier people tend to say Mummy and Daddy. Nobody really knows why...

Pardon- choose Sorry? What? Or excuse me?

Portions- a "helping" of food would sound more upmarket.

Tea- choose dinner or supper instead.

Lounge- refer to it as a drawing room or a sitting room.

Posh. This word is rarely used by the truly, actually posh. The royal family prefer to use the word "smart".

Perfume. This is often simply referred to as scent in wealthier company.

Horses. At a polo match these are customarily referred to as ponies, even though they aren't. Again, no-one really knows why...

Everyday Elegance

Finances with Finesse:

Handling Money

The truly well off can afford to be generous, and generosity is incredibly attractive and signals wealth. However you must work within your means. If you give everything away at the beginning then you won't ever build up the assets to join the ranks of the rich. Be generous in small things. Buy your friend a coffee, cover the tip in the restaurant, and you will create an affluent aura. No one will know that you can't afford the Ferrari, and just maybe, by living within your means, one day you will. Stinginess in small things will mark you out as poor and break the image you wish to project, so don't be miserly.

Whether rich or poor it's considered vulgar to discuss money. Never, ever ask someone their hourly wage, yearly salary, or the cost of their house or car. In fact it's best not to ask about the price of anything at all. Occasionally certain people will be very eager to discuss the cost of their possessions or their wages etc., in which case humour them as they're obviously either proud of it, proud of the bargain they got, or want some sympathy...Always wait for this information to be volunteered by the person themselves however.

When it comes to your own finances you are perfectly free to be enigmatic. A simple polite change of subject or flippant "well now, I can't really remember..." should throw them of the scent. If you are asked directly, and don't mind telling, then it's okay to do so.

If you're lucky enough to be wealthier than most, which some us if we're honest in Western society often are without appreciating it, then never be flash with your money. Some people are struggling to even put food on the table and keep a roof over their families heads, let alone go on a holiday, so it's very insensitive to rub your wealth in others faces. Some of the nicest, wealthiest people are often surprisingly low key. They have learnt to tone it down because they don't wish to invoke the envy of others or draw attention to others smaller means.

If you are wealthier than your companions then there is some element of noblesse oblige. You should be thoughtful of them, and suggest venues and activities you know they can afford. If you yearn for the high life and need them to accompany you, don't make them feel bad or overspend as they are too embarrassed to decline, instead make it your treat and offer to pay for them.

Mixing Friendship and Finance

Always help out your friends with money if it's an emergency, of course, but on the whole try not to mix friendship with money. Only ever lend a friend what you could stand to lose, and forgive them for if they forget to pay you back. It's easier not to bear a grudge over a smaller amount, and prevents otherwise valued friendships floundering because of built up resentment over money.

On the flip side, make sure you never end up in the debt of others too much, as it is sadly all too easy to forget to repay, especially in the case of smaller amounts, here and there- which although may not seem significant at the time, will soon add up- and may not be forgotten so readily by the lender. Make a habit of carrying a modest amount of cash on your person everyday so you don't have to borrow when unexpected things come up.

If you do find yourself in a position where you owe money, always pay it back, and try to do so promptly enough so that they don't have to ask you for it- which is embarrassing for both parties. Amongst good friends, it's often more civilised to keep a tally of debts on a more "like for like" basis I.e. they paid for your meal and drinks when you were short, so you offer to take them out to dinner next month. This turns the whole experience into something altogether more positive.

If someone insists on treating you to something expensive and you know realistically that you will neither be able to, nor be expected to pay them back, such as a mini break, try to pay them back in kind. Perhaps you can buy the odd meal or drink here and there, a spa experience at the hotel maybe. Try to show your gratitude in small ways, despite your more modest means.

To Tip or Not to Tip

Tipping varies from country to country. In Britain you can tip if you want to, it's a nice gesture if you were pleased with the experience, but not expected, and don't worry too much about calculating a percentage, even a pound or two will suffice. In America tipping is expected unless you have received terrible service, and in fact many wait staff rely upon it to top up their wages. Risk looking mean if you don't. Remember tipping can be customary at varying levels and for differing services in different countries, so it's polite to carry out a little online research before you arrive so that you can fall in line with the locals.

The Art of Giving and Receiving

It's lovely to receive gifts, and for the more gracious, just as lovely to give them. The area of gift giving and receiving can present certain pitfalls however, turning joyous occasions into slightly perplexing ones. Avoid these pitfalls by paying attention to the following simple rules:

- **If you're visiting someone else's house for more than a simple cup of tea etc., always bring a gift with you**. The size and type of gift will depend on the occasion, and also your budget. Remember home made is just as good, if not better, as it's personal and took time to make. For a casual drinks meet up, a bottle of wine or some nibbles is quite sufficient, just a little something to bolster the provisions; but if you know that the host or hostess has gone to some trouble, a bunch of flowers or good quality chocolates is appropriate. If the gathering is in honour of a birthday, christening, or similar, then a more personalised, occasion specific gift may be required.

- Christmas gift giving in the office is often facilitated through "Secret Santa" nowadays, which helps enormously, particularly as a budget is set in advance- preventing dilemmas about how much you should be spending etc. Try to put some thought into it, furtively enlist the help of someone who knows them better if you are really stuck. Don't be cheap, make sure the gift is worth the budget. Although judicious use of "two for one" gift offers etc. can be employed with impunity. Slightly under budget gifts can be bulked up with sweets, chocolates, alcohol miniatures, toiletries or even novelty socks. Resist the urge to go over budget by more than a few pounds, even if you're wealthy. This is unsportsmanlike and makes others gifts look bad.

- Never buy size dependent items for people you don't know very well, as this could embarrass them if the gift doesn't fit. Joke gifts should be inoffensive, and only attempted if you know the recipient well enough to make such a joke. All rules go out of the window of course if you know someone really well and share a banterous kind of relationship, but do remember the gift will probably be opened in public, and sooner or later, most items get sleuthed back to their original source, especially the more memorable ones...

- Often offices will also have a "birthday club" or some such thing, which solves the awkward problem of birthday gifts. If yours doesn't, maybe suggest one, or try to be tactful about selectively giving gifts to your favourite colleagues or work friends. Either give gifts to everyone, or do it quietly when you are alone with the recipient. This prevents others from feeling left out or unpopular.

- Cash gifts are a very nebulous area, and whether you should do it or not depends very much on the receiver and your relationship to them. As a general rule, don't do it, unless you are specifically asked, *(such as in the case of a honeymoon fund or similar)*, or are significantly older than them and related. Younger relations, old enough to visit shops, usually absolutely love receiving money above all else and usually have zero shame about it too. So don't hold back! Be that favourite Auntie or whatever...But for everyone else, stick to traditional gifts, so as not to embarrass or offend the recipient. If you feel that they would appreciate the chance to choose their own gift however- consider a gift card.

- Gift cards are always welcome, although they can be a bit of a cop out in some instances. Feel free to buy a gift card if you really can't think of anything more personal or if you would have liked to have given them cash but don't want to embarrass them. Actually sometimes they can be a god send. A hard up friend for example, who might feel patronised by cold hard cash, would most likely be delighted with a multi-store gift card.

- If someone ever buys you a gift and you don't have one for them, don't panic! Keep the situation positive by not drawing attention to your lack of gift. Concentrate instead on lavishing thanks and appreciation on the gift giver. This will make them feel good, and unless they are incredibly immature, they will remember this feeling far more than your giftless-ness. If you wish to, buy them something and send it along afterwards- you can always tell some small white lie, such as you forgot to bring it with you or you were late with your Christmas shopping this year.

- Re-gifting is terrible and you should never do it...Seriously, just make sure your crime is never found out- you'd be surprised how many circles of acquaintance overlap in unexpected ways, especially on social media. It's safe to do this with a generic bath and body gift, but never risk something more unusual or personal.

- Thank you notes for gifts are often overlooked nowadays, particularly handwritten ones, so this is one small area in which it is easy to distinguish oneself and earn the reputation of being very well mannered. For a small gift, an email or text thank you is fine. Go full on card or notelet and best handwriting for a larger gift.

- Remember, giving a gift isn't just about what's inside the wrapping. Consider the whole experience as part of the present. Take the time to label it carefully and wrap beautifully in coordinated paper, to bring anticipation right from the very beginning. Don't be one of these people who throws their offerings unlabelled and unwrapped into a random gift sack inherited from someone else last Christmas.

House Guest Dos and Don'ts

When visiting someone else's house for a dinner or drinks party there are some things you MUST do, and some you definitely shouldn't...There are two types of guest in the world, although many of us fall somewhere in between- the perfect guest, and the guest from HELL! Which one are you?

The perfect guest:

- RSVP's
- Turns up in time, neither too late nor too early, with a bottle of wine or some other drink and a small gift such as nibbles or flowers. (Offer to help put the flowers in a vase).
- They are appropriately dressed in lovely clothes to bring some sparkle to the party.
- Makes an effort to speak to everyone, especially the wallflowers, and is positive and enthusiastic.
- Offers to help the host- to pour, to serve, or to clear up afterwards.

- Toasts the host and compliments the food. As a bare minimum, says nothing if the food is appalling- unless its dangerously unfit for consumption.
- Neither overstays their welcome nor leaves too early (leaving others to suspect they may have somewhere else they'd rather be).
- Makes a point of thanking the host and saying goodbye to them as they leave. At smaller gatherings you should take your leave of everyone else present too. Don't be afraid to briefly interrupt conversations to do so.
- Sends at least a thank you text message or short email the next day. If it was a more formal event requiring more work then you may wish to send a proper card through the post.
  - **Do this!**

The guest from hell...

- RSVP's late or never.
- Turns up either really late or really early when the host is still getting ready. Sometimes doesn't even bother to show up at all to eat the meal which has been lovingly prepared for them.
- Doesn't make any kind of effort with their clothes and dampens the atmosphere.
- Brings no drink and no gift. If a gift is offered, it's the cheapest most awful thing they could find at the last minute.
- Claims the undivided attention of the host or particular friends all evening and makes no effort to include others.
- Turns up drunk or smokes everywhere in a non smoking household.
- Turns up with a whole gang of uninvited associates.

- Declines the hosts cooking efforts or makes faces when they eat it.
- Drinks everything in sight, especially the more expensive bottles.
- Starts arguments, hits on other peoples partners, or watches TV all evening.
- Doesn't take a hint and never leaves until long after everyone else has gone- maybe even falling asleep on the sofa.
- And doesnt even condescend to thank the host the next day for the mayhem they have wrought upon their household...
  - **Don't do this!**

Smart Smoking

Smoking is falling out of favour, and it would be remiss of me to neglect to mention that it's an inelegant pastime to indulge in. Putting the obvious health concerns aside, there are so many reasons why smoking is in conflict with a Ladylike image.

Nicotine stained fingers and a cigarette hanging out your mouth just aren't a good look. Then there's the smell, the unsociability of it all as the smokers clique head outside, and the general stigma.

It's horribly aging. Everyone knows it's bad for you. Vaping isn't much better, although a great improvement.

But I'm not here to judge. If you're a smoker then there are ways you can keep the non smoking majority sweet.

Smoking Commandments:

1. Thou shalt ask if those nearby mind you lighting up.
2. Thou shalt never smoke in a non smokers house or car.

3. Thou shalt not blow smoke at others and should take account of wind direction.
4. Thou shalt perform perfunctory checks for children or pregnant women before lighting up.
5. Thou shalt limit smoking breaks at work, as others generally view these as extra breaks.
6. Thou shalt never take a smoke break during dinner but wait until after pudding.
7. Thou shalt always use an ashtray. Never a used plate, flowerpot, or other unidentified vessel in someone's house.
8. Thou shalt not burn people or furniture.
9. Thou shalt smoke elegantly. The cigarette should never be unsupported in your mouth and it should be removed before you speak.
10. **Social Smokers:** Thou shalt not always cadge cigarettes off the same person, unless drinks are bought in recompense.

A little note for non smokers: Even if you really hate smoking, it's not polite to huff and puff and cough and lecture. You may have the moral high ground here, but it's just not nice to cause a scene, especially as many smokers would desperately love to quit if they could. If it's outside and not on your property, just move away.

Elegant Inebriation

Inevitable as it sometimes is in life, getting blind drunk (*or worse, high*!) is the very opposite of elegant. Nor is puking your guts up in the club toilet, or horrors, the taxi! Ideally try not to do it. If you do succumb, ensure as a bare minimum that you're in loyal and conscientious company, who care enough to reign in the more risky antics of their companions. Be a conscientious friend yourself- keep an eye on your friends, and in return they will hopefully keep an eye on you.

Try to remain in the safe, happy zone of lightly delightful tipsiness. Employ tricks such as never drinking on an empty stomach, pacing your drinks, and avoiding shots and those other kinds of dangerously effective, inelegant concoctions often enjoyed by students...You know the ones! If you wish to appear sophisticated, choose wine, champagne (*if the budget allow*s), otherwise prosecco, or perhaps a classic cocktail such as a gin and tonic.

If you plan to overindulge, stick to the same genre of drink in an evening, either wine, spirits, cider or beer, to reduce your chances of being inelegantly sick. *(And also lessen the severity of the hangover the next morning!)*

If you're tempted to drink to cover nervousness, to become more entertaining, or because you just genuinely dislike socialising, remember that this is wont help you in the long run. It will only mask your problems and hinder true growth of character. Charisma and poise in society can be developed with practise, even by the most introverted. Consistently using alcohol as a crutch might mean eventually you find it hard to function without it, which is an unhealthy and unglamorous way to socialise. Try to be brave, and if parties are really not your thing, don't force it. Concentrate on building a social life based around other activities instead.

Try to always leave the soiree a little too soon, rather than a little too late. Be the friend everyone wishes stayed longer, rather than that over emotional drunkard who is always lingering at the bitter end of every party.

If the worse comes to the worst, as at some point it may well do, and you behave badly while drunk, practise immediate damage limitation the next morning. Text or phone any offended parties immediately, buttering them up with contrite flowers or offers to replace damaged items as appropriate. Most people are very forgiving of drunken mistakes, because most of us have at some point been there ourselves- so don't overthink it, but do reach out to make amends. Remember, at some time in the future, you'll probably all look back and laugh.

If other people get drunk and make fools of themselves, its kind to refrain from plastering their mistakes all over social media, tempting though it may be...Hopefully they will, in return, allow you the same courtesy. If not; laugh it off, roll your eyes, resolve to be better, and if possible cajole the offending poster to take the picture down. Being all grumpy and dramatic about it will only prolong the memories. If nothing else, make sure you've untagged yourself so it doesnt appear connected to your name and be searchable by prospective employers. You will certainly get over small humiliations, maybe even outgrow some friends, but the internet is eternal...

Conflict Management and parting ways

Not all friendships will last forever, and this is not necessarily a bad thing. By cutting out a bad or unfruitful branch in your life you can make room for more rewarding entanglements. You must aim for the path of least pain and embarrassment for the friend concerned however, and the least damaging for your poised reputation. To this end, it's usually best to employ the "freeze" tactic. Simply freeze them quietly out of your life. Don't return their messages, and if you have the misfortune to bump into them in public, quietly excuse yourself- you're ever so sorry you have to go because someone is waiting for you, you've been very busy etc.

Sometimes in life you may have to have an inevitable confrontation of some kind. On these occasions it's best to do it in a public place to discourage screaming or worse, preferably with another unemotionally involved friend to adjudicate. If at all possible, conduct the confrontation via email or phone, and sleep on what you have written in case you're having an emotional over reaction. Showdowns are only really ever worth the drama and gossip if you genuinely would like to repair the friendship and can't move forward without one. If you just want them out of your life for good, protect your dignity and go for the "freeze"...

Dating Dilemmas

Ideally, love affairs should be wonderfully organic, soul fluttering things- where no etiquette rules are needed. They spring from the heart, and as the dynamics of every couple are so different- to be in love is to be in a lawless rose-tinged country all of your own. So on the whole it's best to leave this secret intimate world free from the dictates of etiquette. For if you can't truly be your authentic sometimes imperfect self with your life partner, when can you be?

However it's at the very beginnings and endings of relationships that little dilemmas may present themselves. Such as what to do on the first date, how to let someone down gently, or at the regretful end of an affair, how say goodbye. For these awkward occasions, certain standards of decency should be maintained.

First date:

It hardly needs to be said, but make an effort with your appearance and personal hygiene- you never know, he could be the love of your life! There's a fine line between making an effort and looking desperate however, so get a second opinion from an ally if you're not sure. For first dates in informal restaurants or coffee shops, Smart Casual is your friend.

Offer to split the bill, and make sure that you have the means to do so. Most likely if he's a gentleman he will offer to pay, in which case you should gracefully accept.

You may or may not have opinions on whether you will see him again if he actually takes you up on it and splits the bill. This is your prerogative, but do pay your share all the same or you'll give the impression that you only came out for a free dinner.

Dating can be expensive and there are plenty of promising *young* men or students with genuinely slim wallets, so when you're thinking about whether to see him again consider whether he made you feel special in other ways. Is he broke, progressive, or just cheap? It's an important distinction.

Sometimes men who are "flash" with the cash can be emotionally poor, buying a woman to excuse their shoddy behaviour in other ways. Judge him fairly as entitlement is just as unattractive as cheapness. Also be cautious as decent, honourable wealthy men have options and often highly developed radars when it comes to gold diggers. If he suspects you're more interested in his money than him, he'll run a mile.

Keep conversation light and friendly. Be interested in him, but don't overshare details of ex boyfriends, marriage fantasies, baby longings, extreme politics, bad behaviour etc. These conversations are important but should come further along the line.

If you like him, then let him know with smiles, light touches, open body language and prolonged eye contact. If the vibe is right, talk about things you could do together or share, use "we"- *"Wow, we seem to like the same kinds of music!"* etc. Make it easy for him to imagine planning another date with you.

If you don't like him, be pleasant, but try not to lead him on. It may be tempting to get tipsy and over friendly, especially if nervous- but this can lead to lady "beer goggles"- *wine goggles*?. The first date ought ideally to be undertaken relatively sober for optimal intelligence gathering.

For a first encounter, it's best to keep it short and sweet. If you're having a wonderful time then of course continue, but it's always good to leave on a high rather than dragging it out, so try to read the room. It can be useful to have a plausible get out clause for when you're ready to leave- popping in to see your friend on the way home, for example, or an early morning activity the next day.

Bad behaviour is never excusable, and in this case, you owe them nothing. Never be afraid to leave an unacceptable date- etiquette rules are to be torn up here.

After the date it's more sophisticated to wait for him to contact you first. If he doesnt and you really liked him, try a short message a few days later letting him know you had fun and would be open to seeing him again. If you still hear nothing, well it's his loss. Don't contact him again.

There are silly rules still floating around certain corners of the dating world saying a man should wait three days after a first date before he contacts a woman, so don't be too surprised if you don't hear from him immediately. He may have fallen for these rules, much like women sometimes play hard to get. *(Only effective in moderation. Quality men won't appreciate games.)*

A sensible man who is truly smitten is generally much quicker to get in contact however. Always remember if they're not super attentive at the beginning, it's only going to lessen as the relationship progresses. Know your worth. Maximum male enthusiasm levels from the offset save heartbreak in the long run. You can encourage attraction to grow, but you can't manufacture it from nothing.

To Bed or not to Bed?

This really depends on whether you're looking for fun or a committed relationship. If you just want fun then as long as it's safe, consensual, and discrete then go for it!

Emphasis on **discrete**. A ladies "black book" should operate on a strictly need to know basis- and no strings attached escapades if they are indulged in should take place out of town or on holiday, and certainly not in your own social circle.

At the risk of sounding old fashioned, if you're looking for a serious relationship possibly leading to marriage with a high quality man, then it's best to channel the spirit of Anne Boleyn somewhat and don't jump straight into bed with him on the first date. Of course more leeway is allowed here if you've known each other for a while as friends first. Then it can be quite delicious to succumb at last to the growing attraction...

Successful relationships have certainly evolved from sex on a first date, but the general message you're giving to the man from this is that you would have done the same thing with any other reasonably amusing and attractive chap who took you to dinner. He is unlikely to refuse the sex, but be warned he may not take you as seriously afterwards, as who wants their wife *(or husband)* to be one of so many? Both men and women want to feel special- they want to feel that they were chosen because of their great qualities, not just because they happened to show up conveniently.

That's not to say we need to be prudish in 2021! Life is for living after all and times have moved on from days past with reliable, easily accessible contraception. However there is a lot to be said for the classic and delightful anticipation of the chase, the frisson of new attraction, and the slow delicious descent into surrender...

Men will act like they prefer instant gratification, but like us women, they often don't know what they really want until it's introduced to them. A poised elegant lady, encouraging their advances yet holding back just a little is able to inspire levels of yearning desire in quality men that ladies who offer it all up straight away "on a platter" never will.

Sensuous looks, light touches, subtle innuendo and a dash of patience will ensure you attract a man who longs for you body and soul and considers you a prize to both win and cherish.

No-Shows

It's unfortunately common in the age of internet dating to be stood up on a date. So first and foremost, try not to take it personally. You're one of many- join the club. Remember you're meeting someone you encountered online- they've not seen you in person before, and they must have liked your pictures or they would never have agreed to a date in the first place. The vast majority of "no shows" are down to either a genuine reason, chickening out or getting drunk, or second thoughts because they're actually still in some kind of relationship with someone else.

So with that being said, what's a girl to do if she finds herself all alone in a bar or restaurant with no date?

1. Keep your cool and try to give them the benefit of the doubt. It's possible that they are just held up or that something bad has happened to them. So refrain from shooting off angry messages, as you'd come off badly if they're in the hospital after crashing on the way or rescuing their grandma from armed robbers. I'm being dramatic, but you get the idea. Benefit of the doubt

should be your first response in any "running late" scenario.
2. If you hear nothing then you should call them, but allow twenty minutes grace before you do. This is a casual date, not a business meeting. Again, benefit of the doubt. On the tiny off chance that this person could be the love of your life and is genuinely held up, showcase your relaxed and understanding personality.
3. After half an hour, if you have not heard back, you are allowed to make a dignified exit. Leave them a short, polite but cool message informing them that you waited for half an hour but as you did not hear from them you have now left the premises. Don't contact them again after this unless you receive a grovelling apology and a genuine sounding reason for their absence.
4. Try not to feel sorry for yourself if you've been ghosted, remember it's really not you, its them. They clearly lack basic manners and you have higher standards than that. If you can, don't waste the nice outfit or the rest of the day, call a friend and go out and have some fun.

Ghosting and Rejection

If you've organised a date and you're tempted to not show up yourself, remember this is terribly bad form. Another person is excited about this date, and has most likely made an effort and cleared their schedule for you.

Nobody is forcing you to go on the date, but please do the honourable thing and let them know in good time if you're not going to be there . Don't wait until they're sitting all alone in a bar or restaurant before you message them. No one wants an audience to witness this kind of rejection.

If you simply cannot make the date for practical reasons, tell them this, and reschedule. If it's something else, like lukewarm attraction or you never want to see them again, it's best to be decisive and as kind as you can. A simple "I'm not looking to be in a relationship right now" or "I like you but don't feel a romantic spark" are kind ways to nip an unwanted suitor in the bud. Even "I've met someone else" or I'm still in love with my Ex" are perfectly inoffensive and useful means for decisively ending short romances. They may or may not be truthful, but in the case of love, which is a very personal thing, never be afraid to employ a little white face- saving lie.

If you're cancelling the date because of nerves, do remember, it's probably now or never, as they're unlikely to show up again if you keep messing them around. Dating is nerve wracking for virtually everybody. Try to be brave and meet them, it's only coffee after all.

Ex Boyfriend

Close proximity of The Ex can be a problem if you share mutual friends or are in the same town and bumping into him is inevitable.

Unfortunately you can't hide from him forever in this situation, so it's best to deal with the very real possibility of meeting him as soon after the break up as you are emotionally able to.

If you're lucky enough to have advance warning of the meeting- a mutual friends party perhaps-prepare yourself. Whether he ended it or you did, as shallow as it sounds, great peace of mind will ensue from knowing that you looked your best when you met. After any breakup it's an unwritten rule that a girl should pamper herself of course- so treat yourself to that new dress and a good haircut.

This is all more about boosting your own confidence than anything else. Never give a man a second chance if he breaks up with you or cheats - except in very unusual instances. Intense family dramas, work stress, mental breakdowns, and illness are possible mitigating circumstances, but only if severe enough *(and genuinely contrite enough)* to warrant your forgiveness.

Quality men aren't complicated. If they respect you and want to be with you, they'll be very clear about it with their actions. Reciprocate enthusiastically, but never chase a man unless asking for forgiveness you don't deserve.

If you run into your ex unexpectedly and it comes as a shock, remember nothing good ever comes from causing a scene. Stun him with your cool politeness and poise. Show him that you are better than that, and by extension, better than him. Success is always the best Revenge.

If there was no foul play on either side, just a drifting apart, then you owe it to him to be kind and courteous. Say hello, ask him how he is, smile...But be careful not to flatter or flirt with him if you suspect he still holds a torch for you.

In an ideal world, you and him hopefully won't have much occasion to meet, unless you're striving for that rarest of things- genuine *friendship* with an ex. Sometimes though, the crossing of paths is inevitable if you live in the same town or share friends. In this case then over time you will have to reconcile yourself to the fact that you will probably have to be at the very least civil, if not friendly, to his new girlfriend. Give her a chance if you're mature enough to bear it, as it will prevent situations where you're put off going out because "she" might be there.

If you really can't cope with seeing him without becoming angry and emotional, avoidance is your best policy. Offload your feelings on a supportive friend and heal in private to preserve your elegant reputation. Never date someone unsuitable just to be seen to be moving on.

Breakups and saying goodbye

Assuming your partner is essentially a good person then you owe it to him to be kind. Don't mistake kindness for dragging it out though. If it's over then you need to let him know.

If the relationship has been of some length then you should meet him in person. Choose a public place if you're worried about him causing a scene or changing your mind with emotional blackmail. If it's a long distance relationship then a phone call is acceptable.

Cheating, or lining his replacement up before you have even separated is very bad form. So is keeping his possessions, which should be returned. Any gift he gave you can be considered yours and kept, with the notable exception of engagement rings, which are traditionally returned to the man- especially if they are family heirlooms.

Texting or emailing to end a relationship is defendable only for the very briefest of liaisons. Having said that, it's always better than nothing if you're feeling cowardly. Never ghost. Give the poor chap some closure.

If the shoe is on the other foot and you are the one being broken up with, try to leave with your pride intact. Crying, tantrums or emotional blackmail will only make you look bad, and any victory at this point is likely to be a shallow one. Men know what they want, and if he doesn't want *you* then there will be plenty of good men who *will*.

If you really want him back then your only chance at this stage is to make him miss you and feel a little jealous as he sees you enthusiastically entering the singles scene again with your friends. *(Remember Kate Middleton hitting the clubs after Prince William split up with her that time..?)* Enthusiasm for life is far more attractive than neediness. Maybe send him a short friendly message in a couple of weeks, after a judicious picture or two on Instagram of you and the girls having fun, trying a new hobby etc. See what happens, but know when to "fold" as they say in poker. Keep your dignity.

Sometimes we have to accept that like us ladies, men sometimes just don't feel that special "spark" with a woman. We often feel the same way, and there's nothing you can do about it. You can't manufacture desire or force someone to love you.

Often people get into relationships because the initial attraction is there but later find that they don't have a lot in common. Men, being very visually stimulated creatures can be prone to this- which does provide some bolster for the argument of not jumping straight into bed with a man too soon if you're looking to find a proper relationship!

You can rest assured that if he dated you, he found you attractive. It's more likely a compatibility issue which doomed the relationship. So don't take it to heart. You're a beautifully unique lady- and your prince charming is out there somewhere...

Society Occasions and Outings

Restaurant Courtesies

Always phone or book online ahead if you're planning on going out to eat in a quality restaurant. Not only does this prevent disappointment but in some establishments it may get you a better table, as many people don't bother to book and the serving staff will most likely allocate you a good table if you have taken the time to let them know in advance. If you're looking to be even surer of getting one of the best spots in the house, you could try asking them to recommend you the best table when you ring to book. Alternatively, if it's true, or if you are feeling cheeky, you could subtly slip in that it is for a special occasions. Don't be surprised if better restaurants then proceed to bring out a cake and candles though!

As with any prior engagement it's important to be on time to your booking. Even more so if you are the host and have invited others, in which case you should aim to be the first to arrive. Five minutes is neither here nor there in the restaurant world, but do let the restaurant know if you are likely to be longer. Other guests might have booked the table for later so they might need some advance warning to free up another table in time. If you're very late and don't let them know, expect to find your table taken by someone else. Restaurants are a business after all.

If you've expressly invited someone out to dinner (rather than just generally agreeing to go out as a group or pair,) then pay for them, and be prepared for them to choose what they like from the menu. It pays to make sure that the establishment is within your means ahead of time rather than having to embarrassingly ask your guest for their share. On the other hand, If you've been invited out by someone else, come prepared to pay even though hopefully you won't have to, and try to choose modestly. You don't have to order the cheapest item on the menu, but neither should you go straight for the most expensive either. Arguably though, if you know the person to be wealthy and you genuinely really want it, you get a free pass- order that filet mignon and the caviar!

When you enter a better restaurant you may find that the wait staff approach you to pull out your chair for you or take your coat. Accept this old fashioned gesture of civility with good grace, as thought to the manner born, and never grab at the chair. Wait for it to be pulled out and then seat yourself gently down.

Secure drinks, but don't rush to order food immediately. Others may have entered the restaurant before you and this will cause anxiety for the serving staff, as other guests who may have been waiting longer will get annoyed if you are seen to "queue jump".. You shouldn't have to wait more than ten minutes for attention however. Closing your menus on the table when the whole party have chosen should be enough to attract service. After this if no one appears, feel free to summon the waiter with a little wave, an "excuse me", and a smile. Never click your fingers as seen in some old movies. It's horribly entitled, and offending anyone responsible for your food is never going to be a good idea.

Occasionally older gentlemen may ask what you want and then try to order for you. It's best to humour them. You can't always teach old dogs new tricks, and they mean well. Some women enjoy this, of course.

Don't be that resident vulture who steals other peoples food. Ladies can sometimes be guilty of this, ordering a salad when they really wanted the loaded fries...Most will be too well bred to refuse you, but inside they may be resentful. If you're hungry, order your own! It's sometimes sweet to swap tastes of desert if you're in very intimate or romantic company, but make sure that its reciprocal, and keep it low key.

Politely mention issues such as dirty cutlery, raw meat etc. to the wait staff. You're not being difficult and fussy by refusing to eat dangerous or unhygienic food. The polite amongst us usually don't want to make a big deal for trifling issues though. Sometimes it's more tactful to grin and bear it if you're someone's guest, so as to maintain the geniality of the evening. In real situations however, and at the last resort, ask to speak to the manager. Remember it is in their interest to keep you happy and not cause a scene, so if you remain pleasant the issue will most likely be settled to your advantage.

At the end of the meal, don't forget to tip if you want to and have had good service (or if you are in America). Tipping is not essential in Britain but it shows good breeding and awareness of the often relatively unimpressive wages of wait staff. Ironically, many British people will tip in a larger restaurant where they are on show but not bother in a more modest restaurant where the wages are even lower. Don't bother in fast food restaurants however as you're tipping the service staff not the chef or the food itself.

No doggie bags. These should only be requested by people who are truly counting their pennies, and are as such a bad look, as well as an additional chore for busy staff. Old reheated food is never quite the same anyway. Try to order only what you know you can eat- greed becomes no one and is a poor show when so many in the world go hungry.

You don't have to shoot off the second you have put down your fork, but do remember time is money in the restaurant business. To linger for hours afterwards hogging the table and buying nothing is thoughtless. If you've all finished but the conversation is still lively, order another round of drinks to buy yourselves some more time. Eventually you may need to retire to a nearby bar or club.

Suavely Settling the Bill

Never mix business and pleasure is the old adage, and never can this ring truer than when groups of friends attempt to sort out the bill after a meal out. All sorts of issues can arise. Someone, who doesn't have a lot of money and ordered a salad wishes they could just pay for their own, someone else suggests splitting the bill equally, some other generous soul wants to pay for the whole lot but naturally no one is going to let them do it. Of course, the kindest thing for the restaurant staff would be for one person to pay, and then for the others to pay them back, preventing a whole host of separate bill's, but of course it's not always possible to do it that way.

In a nutshell though, the rules of etiquette dictate that you should never, ever quibble over a bill. Ideally expectations should have been laid out between friends casually beforehand, a simple "we'll split the bill equally, right? Or are we each getting our own?" should be sufficient to lay the cards out on the table before the bill arrives and confusion ensues.

Actually though, in civilised company the bill is normally split equally between all the members of the party. This is not fair, necessarily, as each person will have ordered different menu items with varying price points. However, if money is not considered a big deal as the party are all comfortably off, this is a sensible way of doing things as it just makes the maths so much easier. To work it all out individually down to the nearest penny can be a headache, and seems ungenerous and pernickety unless you genuinely are living from wage check to wage check; and if times are that hard, you have to question whether you should be eating out at all. Stay at home and look for a better job!

There is an argument to be made for pardoning the designated driver from some of their share of the bill. This is to thank them for their kindness, their petrol, and also out of respect for the fact that alcoholic drinks are significantly more expensive than soft ones- and will likely mount up over the evening.

Early leavers of the meal should make absolutely sure that they leave enough to cover their bill. It's better to err on the generous side here and leave slightly more than you think it will be, as it's a much better look. If you really have no idea what it will be, having a quiet word with a friend to say that they must let you know afterwards if you owe more will save face.

If you invite others to dinner then it is your job to pay for them. It's also your job to cover the tip. There is a difference though of course between expressly inviting people/someone out to dinner and just merely suggesting you should go to dinner. Be clear about what you mean, or what you yourself have been invited to, and manage your expectations. If a casual dinner was just suggested by a friend then the bill should be split.

As a host you should never accept when others offer to pay for themselves. As a guest you should always offer to pay, even though you know it will most likely not be accepted. It's a little silly, but it's all part of the social ritual .

Occasionally a senior, clearly more wealthy member of the party may insist on paying, and in this case, their claim trumps the host. Humour them, and accept with grace as it brings happiness to older people who can afford it to cover the bill, particularly when it comes to treating their families. Only accept if it's abundantly clear they have more than enough money to do so though.

Check whether any tip is already included on the bill as a service charge. If not, in America 15-20% of the bill is expected. In the UK, 10-15% would be appreciated, but exact calculations are not expected. Cash is often preferred for tips if available as it ensures it ends up in the pockets of the rightful recipients. Remember you are tipping the quality and attentiveness of the service, not the food itself, which is a matter to bring up with the manager if unacceptable.

Hotel Courtesies

Let the reception of the hotel know if you're going to be significantly late. They shouldn't sell your room to someone else, but it has been known to happen. At the other end of your stay, do your best to check out in time. The check out time isn't an arbitrary time invented to annoy late risers- it's the time the housekeeping staff need to ready the rooms and suites for the next guests. In emergencies there is often some flexibility, another room could be cleaned first for example, but its polite to ring reception and let them know so that they can organise their staffs time. Don't forget that Porters and Bellboys are there especially for the purposes of helping guests with unwieldy luggage, so never feel reticent about summoning one.

If upon reaching your room you find it isn't as promised in the brochure/on the website, you are within your rights to politely let them know. In some cases, you may have to cut your losses, get your money back, and go elsewhere- but in most events if it's a matter of the wrong type of room, the wrong floor, or a terrible view there may be some leeway. By remaining assertive but pleasant you will often find the staff will move heaven and earth to accommodate you. Their reputation is at stake, after all.

Don't come over all rock and roll in your hotel room. It's obvious enough, but breakages and towel stealing etc. may get you on the blacklist. Some people go completely the other way though and spend half their time doing the chamber maids work before they go out in the morning. You don't have to do this. Part of the joy of staying in a hotel comes from not having to do housework, so you're allowed to relax.

When heading to the hotel restaurant for the first time its safer to make more of an effort than otherwise. The higher the stars the hotel has and the higher the prestige, the more likely the restaurant is to be a formal affair with a smart dress code. You may be asked to change if you turn up in jean's, so choose a smart outfit until you have got a feel for the atmosphere of the restaurant- you may well find it's very casual but it's less embarrassing to be the "best in show" rather than scruffy. Besides which, for all anyone knows, you could be heading off to a chic cocktail party after dinner.

If you are misfortunate enough to have noisy neighbours in the next room, take the matter to reception and leave it in their hands. It's best not to get personally involved, no one wants a bad atmosphere on holiday.

Tipping is customary in some hotels for various services, particularly in America. Amounts vary but a safe basic rule could be something like the following:

Porters or Bellboys as they leave the room- one euro, dollar, or pound per case.

Doormen (if providing a service such as calling a taxi cab) – one euro, dollar or pound again.

Room service- two euros, dollars or pounds for food. One euro dollar or pound for drinks.

Housekeeping- a small thank you note would be nice, along with six euros, dollars, or pounds for a short stay. A little more for longer.

These are basic minimum amounts which in some countries will be expected. If you can afford it though and you plan on visiting the hotel again, leave a handsome tip before you leave- and hopefully next time you stay there you will be treated exceptionally well.

The VIP Club: How to Get Past the Velvet Rope

Most clubs will let anybody in... However if you're aspiring to get into somewhere a bit more selective, and remain in there, here are a few tips and tricks which can improve your chances:

- Make an effort, and dress to impress. Every bijoux or higher brow club will have a certain aspirational aesthetic which they aim to exude. If you fit their aesthetic you will have a good chance of being allowed in, particularly as a lady. So do a little research before you turn up on the doorstep. What are their ideal customers on their Instagram/website wearing? What's their vibe? Aim to camouflage yourself so you look like you could be a regular already.
- Large rowdy groups will usually not be let into exclusive clubs. Try to tone it down at the entrance. Hide any glaringly obvious hen party paraphernalia. You might even consider separating to get inside.
- Be polite to the bouncers. Cajole and roll out your best feminine wiles. Don't be aggressive. It's the bouncers job to weed out any possible troublemakers, and if you're already causing mayhem at the door then you'll be a liability inside. Bribery is a last ditch resort, but probably won't work and you'll burn your bridges for next time.
- If you're feeling generous, or have indulged in lollypops or sweets from the toilet attendants pot, then you may want to leave them a small tip. Likewise the cloakroom staff if they have looked after your coat.
- Steer clear of drama once you're inside the club. Try to get pleasantly drunk rather than ridiculously so or your inhibitions will be so lowered that you could get into trouble. Never make moves if there is an obvious girlfriend nearby. Employ the more face saving dancing away across the dancefloor move if someone distasteful is trying their luck. Always rescue a friend in

a similar situation, and never leave a girl down. In the joyous but drunken, crazy atmosphere of a club ladies should look out for each other.
- Don't smoke, drink, or do drugs on the dancefloor. Actually, don't do drugs at all anywhere...Smashed glasses and cigarette burns are no fun.
- Don't hassle the DJ too much for requests. Now and then is fine, but not everyone shares your taste in music.

A note on UV lights

Don't give anyone more of an eyeful than you intend to in the club- UV or strobe lighting will make anything white glow in the dark. So avoid wearing white underwear or under wiring under sheer dresses! Other things which could glow and potentially cause embarrassment include some types of dentistry and even dandruff on dark fabric...

VIP areas

The holy grail of exclusive clubs VIP areas are aspirational but not always as thrilling as they're cracked up to be. However opulent and exclusive the VIP area, most of the energy and atmosphere will be found on the main dancefloors; but if you're lucky enough to be invited over the velvet rope then enjoy moving in and out of the two areas and the slightly envious glances that ensue. Don't go wild with the free bar though, you'll just look very amateur. Likewise, keep your cool if you do encounter a real celebrity or VIP. Asking for autographs or photos will only mark you out as a nuisance and you may not be let in again.

The Opera

General rules which apply to any theatre performance anywhere: Turn off phones, don't chatter through the performance or eat noisy or smelly food. Beware of overdoing the perfume, and unless desperate try to wait until half time until you visit the lavatory. No more than light canoodling at the back.

The opera differs from some performances in that you are not expected, in fact it would be disruptive to applaud after every song. Its easiest to take your cue from other more experienced audience members here, but the general advice is to applaud at the very beginning or at half time as the conductor takes to the stage, and then again at the end of an act, and at the final bows. Spontaneous applause may erupt after a particularly impressive aria, but is generally discouraged at other times.

Since operas often have convoluted story lines and are often sung in Italian, French or German you will probably get more out of the experience if you research the plot a little in advance. Especially if you're in the company of regular opera goers.

Beachside

Even the most casual of scenarios such as a trip to the beach requires a little forethought. Some people abandon all modesty and decorum once there, and it really is a shame. Swim suits are not the most modest of garments, which is perfectly fine of course, but there is a line which you should not cross unless you're literally on a nudist beach.

G strings are rarely a good idea on anyone who isn't a bikini model, and even then, they scream exhibitionist. Grooming of all areas should be thorough, erring on the especially safe side in the case of bikini lines etc. Feet should be pedicured, or at the very least clean and exfoliated, with the nails trimmed. It's a good idea to make it a rule to always bring sun glasses to the beach, as squinting up at the sun is very aging. Make up should be barely there, and where it does make a subtle appearance it should be waterproof. Towels should be clean and neat, and if at all possible, try to coordinate your towel, bag, and sarong.

   Never overcrowd other people on the beach. If at all possible, keep a good distance. This gives you privacy too, so is a win-win situation. Sometimes however, on very crowded beaches you may be left with little choice but to encroach on others- but as a bare minimum keep at least one towel length apart.

   Have fun on the beach, but be courteous to your neighbours, especially if they are close. Try not to make too much noise, or be too ribald, remember beaches are family environments. Save inappropriate topics for later. The shaking of towels should be done carefully so as not to cover your neighbour in flying sand. Watch Frisbees too, no one wants one landing on them if they're trying to relax. Don't stare obviously at others bodies, you'll make them uncomfortable. Sun glasses can be employed to subtly eye up the local talent without detection. Bikinis should only be worn on the sand and in the sea. Cover up with a wrap dress or something similar before you enter shops or restaurants, and never go barefoot. Changing in and out of your swimming costume must be done carefully so as not to give anyone an eye full. Dresses, skirts, sarong, and wrap around towels are useful here as trousers and shorts are very difficult to get in and out of a swimming costume in discreetly.

   Going topless can be liberating but should only be attempted on an appropriately liberated beach or in a very secluded place. It should be a communal activity. Never go topless alone in a group, especially if you're blessed with a beautiful body. Others may secretly resent your exhibitionism or simply feel uncomfortable with it but be too polite to say anything. Keep your legs together on the beach so as not to inadvertently attract perving from the unscrupulous. Similarly, if you're with your significant other try not to get too carried away by the sunshine and skimpy apparel- kisses are okay, but full on make out sessions and more are not a good idea in the daytime. Come back later when the beach is deserted if you're that way inclined.

It's polite to share your provisions, drinks, sun lotion, snacks and games- but do ask yourself before helping yourself to someone else's things. Offering to apply someone else's hard to reach sunscreen is always a kind gesture, and if you're lucky they'll reciprocate.

Be courteous to the environment too. There's that well known saying that goes "take only photographs, and leave nothing but footprints". This is a great philosophy to live by when you visit the beach or anywhere else in nature. There is nothing more obnoxious to the local residents than visitors turning up and leaving old barbeques, cans, and all sorts of rubbish on the beach to harm wildlife. This just gives everyone a bad name. Be respectful and take everything away again. Barbeques should be left to cool and then put into the bin bag you bought with you, but if you're short of time you can pour sea water over them to speed up the process.

Polo Season

There are many types of sporting and outdoor events which could be covered here but Polo stands out as having particular norms and traditions, and as a sport partaken in mostly by the wealthier classes and royalty, many normal people know little about it. If you do find yourself at a polo match, rejoice because it's an excellent opportunity to network with high net worth and influential individuals.

What is Polo? Polo consists of two teams (or Quartets) of four, astride horses with what look like long hockey clubs, called mallets. Each team of four two midfielders, a back, and a forward, or goal striker. The field of play is large, the size of three football pitches, and like in football, the team which scores the most goals through the goalpost at either end of the field wins. After each goal is scored the teams will change ends on the pitch. Each round of play is divided up into seven minutes, called a chukka, the beginnings and end of which are indicated by a hooter.

There are two mounted umpires, dressed in striped shirts. The players themselves will be wearing helmets, knee-pads, and numbered shirts.

It's important to remember that oddly the horses in a polo match are referred to as "ponies" even though they are not. Don't forget to call them ponies if you don't want to show yourself up as a newbie. Polo season is between April and September.

"Divot stomping" is traditional for five minutes at half time. This is just a bit of fun really, a bit of silliness fuelled by champagne. Technically the idea is for spectators to stamp down the turfs kicked up by the ponies to ready the pitch for the next half of the match.

Grandstand seating is where most people will content themselves with sitting. The Members enclosure is where the real high society will be found however- here, instead of picnicking, they will be served with lavish sit down meals and champagne etc on tap.

The dress code is smart casual but with a summery vibe. Polo matches are at their best on beautiful balmy days, where dainty tea dresses, glamorous cover ups, and sunglasses should be worn. Sandals or shoes should be chic but very high pointy heels are impractical and may sink into the grass.

The Private Jet

Private jets are extravagant and bad for the environment. Even the flying habits of royalty come under scrutiny nowadays, and perhaps fairly so when so much energy is used to transport so few people through the sky. However, how many of us, if we're honest wouldn't love to experience the joys of a plane all to ourselves? No queues, no crowds, no hanging around dismal airports, decent in flight food...The benefits speak for themselves.

Expect to have a different experience depending on the size of the private jet, which can vary from relatively modest planes to extravagant, sometimes custom built air palaces.

Dress code should be smart casual- you don't need to dress up, but you should be clean, neat, and simply sophisticated. Towering heels would be inappropriate and sweat pants would somehow not do the occasion justice. Private jetsetters have standards to maintain after all!

You won't have to wait around. Often you'll be expected to present yourself about fifteen minutes before take off, and will then be driven directly to the waiting jet. Don't be late. There will probably be a quick perfunctory baggage check, and a passport check too of course, if you're flying internationally.

Once inside the private jet there are a couple of things to remember:

- Don't distract the pilots at take off or landing. There will generally be a curtain drawn across the cockpit entrance for privacy. However if you are travelling alone then health and safety rules mean that this will not be able to be drawn across- this is so that you can be seen at all times in case of an emergency.

- Remain seated at landing and take off.
- Drinking and smoking may be allowed by your host, maybe even encouraged. Take your lead from them. If you're travelling alone, it's best not to smoke if you're unsure. Drinking should be fine if provided, in fact a drink is often calming for nervous flyers. Just don't over do it and vomit everywhere.

The in flight menu will depend on the size of the plane and its entourage. Smaller cabins may provide quite basic, although good quality food options, which you may have to help yourself to if there are no attendants. Larger planes might have a kitchen and staff, able to whip up whatever you fancy or serve you A la'Carte on proper plates with real knives and forks. No plastic cutlery and pre made food here!

Landing and exiting the airport is just as fabulously straightforward as departure. A car will have been already summoned by the pilot to pick you up on the landing strip for your next destination. You won't have to worry about customs as this will have already been sorted. Blissful!

Remember, onlookers will stare curiously at any private jet and its occupants, so you might want to have a quick freshen up before you ascend from the cabin, so as to not disappoint your audience.

As with any method of transport, leave everything tidy, and don't forget to thank the pilots. If your private jet experience was hosted by someone else, a thank you letter and perhaps a gift would be appropriate too.

The Private Yacht

Sunsets, cocktails on deck, and the blue ocean stretching out endlessly in front of you. Yachting really is the ultimate luxury pursuit. As such, there are rules which you must navigate to make the most of your invitation.

First of all, be clear about exactly what the invitation entails. There are many types of yacht, and therefore many types of yachting experience. Is this a luxury super yacht where your every whim will be catered to by a team of staff, or a more hands on experience on a more modest vessel? Will you be expected to lounge upon the deck in your finery or pull up your sleeves and help? Whilst both are great, albeit in different ways, you do need to know what you are up against so that you can prepare accordingly.

What to pack:

Unless the vessel is particularly palatial then there is unlikely to be a lot of storage space. Now is the time to edit your suitcase to the barest minimum and put together a matching capsule wardrobe of yachting appropriate clothing. Your yachting appropriate clothing stash should include the following items:

- Swimwear- ideally several sets. If it's warm you are going to be wearing this a lot.
- A cover up such as a sarong or wrap dress.
- A waterproof jacket- sporty quick drying sailing ones are best.
- A warm top or two. It can get cold in the evenings on board.
- Sunglasses.
- Deck shoes or appropriately bottomed trainers that won't leave mark's on the pristine deck.
- You may need a cocktail dress or two, depending on the itinerary and trips on shore. Phone ahead to find out as you don't want to use up valuable space if these aren't needed but on the other hand you don't want be left with nothing to wear.

What to expect:

Expect there to be rules on board. Sailing comes with intrinsic hazards and there are certain protocols which must be obeyed for everyone's health and safety. The captain isn't trying to squash anyone's fun or be a dictator, they are just being sensible and attempting to keep everyone alive. On a more modest yacht there may be procedures regarding the toilet (often called the Head), or the shower- due to limited water supplies on board. Heed these as you don't want to use up all the water with your long showers or worse, block the toilet...

Be sensitive to the luxury of the yacht. There may be rules to protect expensive equipment. Don't take it personally if you are asked not to touch or do certain things- try to respect the fact that you are lucky enough to be holidaying on someone's very expensive pride and joy.

How to behave:

Boarding the boat is traditionally accompanied by a cheery "Permission to board please?". Take care when you board, often this will be up a narrow, quite precarious gangway.

Dress appropriately. Stiletto heels are completely unacceptable on boats, both from a balance perspective and a not damaging the deck one. Black or coloured soles on shoes are also ill advised as they can stain expensive surfaces.

Think about the quality of your surroundings. You may be at sea but you must act as though you are in someone's house. Don't drip in your wet swimming costume all over expensive seats or furnishings. Save this for the top deck only. Likewise if you're covered in sun lotion or fake tan try to keep this to yourself rather than leaving unsightly oil slicks in your wake.

The captains word is final. Whether they own the boat or are chartering it you should listen to them and try to be obliging, for everyone's safety.

The closer quarters of a boat call for extra tact and neighbourliness. Be nice and accommodating, and remember the walls of boats are thinner than the walls of houses. Be quiet at night, and absolutely no bitching or loud passionate encounters; you could be overheard. Be thoughtful of neighbouring vessels- late night wild parties in the close quarters of a harbour are highly insensitive.

It's a sad fact of life that some people feel seasick on a boat. This feeling doesn't usually persist more than a few hours, so with patience you can ride it out and enjoy the rest of your trip. If you do feel nauseous employ some damage limitation; position yourself near a toilet or bowl, or even the railing to direct any vomit overboard. Seasoned sailors suggest not retiring below deck at the first sign of nausea- the feeling is likely to pass quicker out in the fresh air, watching the horizon. Never read or stare at your phone if you feel ill or you will make it worse. Crystallised ginger is a traditional remedy for sea sickness which many swear by.

Try to muck in, tidy up, be polite to any staff, and generally help. If you know absolutely nothing about boats then do show an interest, the captain will be only too delighted to teach you- yachting types love to talk about their yachts- but do pick your moment. Sailing, and particularly docking, requires a lot of concentration and care. It's best to keep a low profile and not get under anyone's feet until you are better acquainted with the procedure. You want to be a help, not a hindrance.

Lastly, the fun part, be aware that anyone on a fancy yacht is going to be very much on display. Others will be looking at you, intrigued by the lifestyle, so don't let them or your host down. If ever there was a time for a fabulous bikini and chic sarong, this is it!

Tipping:

On a small yacht this won't be necessary, but on a larger yacht with a crew it is customary to tip the crew. The amount of the tip is usually dependent on the length of the stay and how well they did their job. It is advisable to ask your host how much is appropriate.

Bonus Yacht Fact

On a boat, left is usually referred to as "port", and right is referred to as "starboard". Incidentally when Port is drunk in company at a formal dinner it is always passed to the left. So Port= left.

How to Meet Royalty

Royalty is somewhat of an anachronism in today's modern world. Whether you love it as representing history and a continuation of ancient traditions, or whether you loathe it as an outdated institution- I think it would be fair to say that as an enduring fixture of some societies it deserves at least a modicum of respect. Not blind servitude, but simply appreciation for its place in culture, and for the life of service which the monarch has led.

It's a well compensated and comfortable service to be sure, but one for which they're rarely left alone, and unlike many other celebrities, they can get away with very little indeed. The taxpayer holds their actions and their integrity very much to account. So although they dwell amongst stupendous wealth, heaven forbid if they are shown to be too excessive, too profligate, too frivolous... Indeed, as Katie, the Duchess of Cambridge, or Meghan, the Duchess of Sussex, would probably tell you- if it's just a relaxed life of luxury you dream of, you're probably better off marrying an ordinary billionaire!

When meeting royalty:

If at a formal event, wait to be introduce by a royal side. Don't introduce yourself first. Ideally curtsey, but don't overdo it. A brief nod and bob with your weight on the front foot, will be sufficient. Never bow, that's reserved for men. Remember a sunny smile will excuse even the most atrocious of curtsey attempts. Don't forget to bestow another curtsey when you leave.

As for shaking hands; it's polite not to offer your own hand to shake unbidden, but do take a royal hand, gently, if offered it.

How to address the Queen? At the first instance it's good manners to address the Queen as "Your Majesty". You don't have to keep saying this though, after the first time you can say "Ma'am". This should be pronounced as if rhyming with "jam".

Other members of the royal family should be at the first instance referred to as "Your Royal Highness", and then after this you can say "Ma'am" again, or "Sir".

In formal conversations with royalty, unless you know them very well indeed, it's customary to never refer to them in conversation as "you". For instance, rather than saying "Are you enjoying the Flower Show?" you should say "How is Your Royal Highness enjoying the flower show?"

If you are in a position of responsibility at the place of the royal visit you may be requires to introduce others to the visiting royalty. In this instance, you would say something to the effect of "Your Royal Highness/Your Majesty/ Ma'am, may I present Sarah Brown."

It's best at first to allow the conversation to be led by the member of the royal family you are meeting. It shows respect, and they are well used to making others feel at ease in their company. After all, it's their job. Don't be afraid to gently volunteer a little more information yourself if the conversation is going well though.

In more informal situations, perhaps a chance meeting in a restaurant, it's still best to wait to be introduced. Loiter as closely as you can of course, in hope's of an introduction, but don't disturb them, and keep it low key. Causing a scene will only ensure they are whisked away by their aides and out of your sight very quickly.

We are dealing particularly with the British royal family in this book, but if you are lucky enough to meet a member of a foreign royal family, do a little prior research if you're able to. If it is an important event, such as they are to be in attendance at a function you are involved with then there should be a dedicated person in the entourage of the royal household whom you should contact to discuss protocol before the visit.

How to Meet Celebrity

Unlike royalty, celebrities are not obliged to be polite to you, so if you approach them unbidden be prepared for a possible frosty reception. There could even be a body guard lurking nearby if they're on the A list, so approach them cautiously. If the stars are in your favour then they might be having a good day and might even chat or condescend to let you take a picture, but do appreciate that celebrities are not public property and are entitled to be left alone if they're not in the mood.

Actually the most polite thing to do is to ignore them if you possibly can. Especially if they are with their families. If you absolutely must, smile and wave, and if you really think you can get away with it discreetly take a picture from a distance on your camera.

If you do have the chance to have an actual conversation with a celebrity, resist the urge to be over familiar. You may see them on television or YouTube all the time. If you're a dedicated fan you maybe even know lots of random details about their lives, but showing off your knowledge will only ever be very creepy indeed, however well meant.

Similarly, if the celebrity you are meeting plays a famous character, try to refrain from shouting out their characters catchphrase at them. Or worse, asking *them* to say it. They've heard it all before, thousands of times, and it must get tiresome. If you must chat, try to come up with something a bit more original, or make some innocuous conversation about the surroundings or the weather. Treat them respectfully, but like a normal human being- so few people will that it might be refreshing for them.

If you've met them before then don't expect them to remember you. They won't. Try to understand that well known people meet a sea of fans every day and it's only human that they won't recall most of them. The meeting might have been incredibly memorable for you but it was just another moment in their busy public life for them.

If you're meeting celebrities on a more up and close basis such as through your work, be professional. Show respect and interest, but try not to be overawed, and above all, be discrete. Don't ask them too many personal questions and refrain from flexing too much on social media, however tempting. Post what they have agreed to in a professional capacity and no more. If they feel they can trust you, you're more likely to be asked to work with them again.

Entertaining and Hospitality

The Brilliant Hostess

The secret of being the perfect hostess is knowing that there is no such thing as a perfect hostess. Planning is key, and will give your soiree every chance of success, but the real heart of a good party is in its ambiance and atmosphere- and these are natural organic elements which cannot be controlled, only gently encouraged. So do relax, and don't overthink your role as hostess. Nothing is more atmosphere dampening than a control freak, spending half the party stressing out in the kitchen, or wandering around tidying up after guests the moment they put down their plate even for a second or drop a few crumbs. A relaxed host is a charming host.

Set the party off to a good start by letting guests know what to expect before the event. The tone of the party will be set by the manner of the invitation, so if you intend it to be a formal, high end affair send luxury printed cards requiring an RSVP. More informal gatherings better suit an email or a text- but do ensure a little advance warning if you want to make sure most of your guests can make it. Remember, plans are often made a week in advance, even for informal meet ups. The initial invitation is the time to mention the dress code, if applicable.

If you want to throw a memorable event, aim for a varied selection of guests. The best parties combine the cosy laughs of established friendships with the frisson of new people and/or romantic possibilities. As the host, a get together can be a great subtle way to match make for your friends or casually engineer a closer acquaintance for yourself.

Before guests arrive, set the scene and prepare. Start early and make sure you are ready when guests arrive. Tidy up, of course. Fumigate any dodgy areas. Put away any expensive treasures you don't want broken, and lock away any secrets. If necessary you can lock rooms which you wish to remain private. Of course, it's very bad manners to go sniffing around other peoples houses uninvited, but there will always be some who do so, whether through bad manners or simply being tipsy and getting lost looking for the loo.

If guests bring gifts with them, accept them graciously. Flowers should be put into a vase as soon as possible, not just abandoned forlornly at the entrance. It's perfectly acceptable for you not to choose to open the guests gift of wine etc. These can be taken away and put into the fridge or cellar. If someone is thoughtful enough to bring chilled champagne however, then do take the hint- put it on ice- or in the fridge at least- and open it before dinner when all of the guests have arrived as a digestif to get the party started.

As the hostess you have a responsibility at the beginning of the party to make people feel at easy and welcome in your home. Wear nice clothes to add to the ambiance. Greet everyone enthusiastically. Tell them how happy you are that they have come, take their coats, and direct them to where they can get a drink. As the night goes on and the party becomes more established the conviviality will continue more naturally and you can relax, but at the beginning, try to circulate. Introduce people who may not know each other, rescue people who look a little lonely and lost, and just generally try to diffuse any awkwardness caused by not knowing where to go and what to do.

Anyone who is contemplating organising a party should mentally prepare themselves to accept small damages with equanimity. Remember, the most memorable, joyous parties are often a little bit wild and free...A bit of cleaning and an occasional breakage are often the price you pay for a great party. Just make sure anything truly valuable is packed away safely beforehand- and if the worst happens, try to refuse offers of compensation unless you truly can't live without it or the friendship will be irreparably damaged on your side without it.

If you have concerns about drugs due to the nature of your particular crowd then it's a good idea to make sure everyone knows about your particular stance on them beforehand. Drugs are not a good look, however you may choose to turn a blind eye to some softer types of drug so as to not cause drama. Always try to manage expectations beforehand if you can to avoid unpleasantness. You owe it to yourself because sadly but inevitably as hostess you're responsible for cleaning up any vomit etc. Or temporarily rehoming passed out guests on the sofa or spare room. Or calling an ambulance and bearing the shame if it all goes very wrong.

If guests are lingering past their welcome and you are desperate to claim your house back and go to sleep, then first of all, take this as a compliment- guests who have settled in are guests who have felt very comfortable and are still enjoying themselves! So don't leave a bad taste in anyone's mouth after an excellent party by unceremoniously kicking them out. It's best to take a softly, softly approach with a well timed yawn or two, by mentioning an appointment you have the next morning, or by asking pleasantly if they would like you to call a taxi. As a last ditch attempt, offer them a nightcap "one for the road" or a mug of cocoa, and slowly but ostentatiously start to tidy up. If you really can't shift them, just go to bed with a cheery wave. They'll probably get the message...

Cocktail Party

Drinks parties are usually casual affairs, and are a great way for the beginner to test the soiree holding waters. They can be very simple, casual affairs, but can also be very Chic, depending on how much work you want to make for yourself.

Guests are going to be drinking, so don't forget the snacks to line their stomachs! Canapés are a very fluid concept. They can be eye wateringly luxurious, incredibly simple, or both of these things at the same time. Think cold, bite sized finger food for maximum ease- these can be prepared well in advance, or even bought in. Always over cater and make sure you have more than you think you will need. Get out the plates. Provide napkins, and well defined places to dispose of olive pips or shells etc. The food should be laid out prettily on a table right in the heart of the party. Feed generously but don't feed the five thousand (unless there ARE five thousand). Remember grossly overfed guests will be sleepy and slow, so you will kiss goodbye to any sparkling conversation.

When it comes to the drinks, which are arguably the focus of a drinks party, you must be generous. Guests may bring their own bottles, but you should make sure that you are not depending on it, as some may not, or some may bring chocolates or flowers instead.

The full spectrum of tastes should be provided for. Of course, you know your friends tastes very well, however in more mixed company aim for white wine, red wine, maybe a rose wine, beer, cocktails and soft drinks. To save yourself work and keep the atmosphere informal you may choose to have a small "do it yourself" mini bar area. Here you would find the basics of spirits, garnishes, ice, glasses, and some mixers so people can make a small variety of classic cocktails for themselves. Alternatively, you could make up a couple of varieties of large pitchers of cocktail.

Set the scene to encourage maximum mixing and fun. Move chairs around to create possible dancing areas and create cosy nooks with atmospheric lighting for intimate chats. Put out ashtrays if necessary and open wine to breathe. Also, consider where guests are going to leave their outerwear. Do you have a cloakroom? If not, you'll need somewhere to put peoples coats, even if it's just on the back of a chair in the hallway.

Start the party with a bang by considering inviting a couple of close friends to help you get ready a little before the main guests arrive. This will give the illusion of atmosphere in that awkward time when the party is just beginning.

Music is an integral part of a fantastic party, so you should plan ahead. Sort out some of your favourite music- perhaps create a playlist with your favourite tunes and some fun crowd pleasers. Think of others though and don't dominate the music if your tastes are a bit niche. It's often fun to delegate and let others take over for a bit here to mix things up and match the developing mood of the party.

If you can afford it and want to really impress, consider outsourcing the catering to a professional company and hiring waiting staff.

Scintillating Dinner Parties

A formal dinner party is a real chance to go all out, to sparkle, to organise and curate the kind of evening you'd love to be invited to yourself. The secret of a great dinner party however is striking a fine balance between doing things properly and being insouciantly relaxed; because however beautiful your decor, however luxurious your food offerings, the real thing that guests will remember is the atmosphere and how welcome they felt in your home.

With this in mind remember that the company is more important than the food. So talk to your guests- don't spend all evening slaving in the kitchen or constantly scurrying back and forth. Facilitate this by considering offering some "made ahead" elements which you can either serve cold or simply reheat on arrival.

When prepping for your dinner party, think about the decor. It's best to work around what you already have, rather than completely reconstructing your dining room. Relaxed, unpretentious luxury is very in anyway, so it would be passé to overdo it. Think beautiful pressed linen napkins in simple shapes, equally beautifully pressed tablecloths, perhaps an elegant minimal spray of flowers. Everything should be clean and sparkling, with personality injected playfully but with the lightest of touches. Too much of anything is just...too much. Far better to concentrate on the quality of the ingredients and their provenance. (For instance, a dinner party isn't the time for the instant coffee granules, it's the time for the artisan ground locally sourced coffee beans etc.)

Consider the seating and whether you have enough room to comfortably house all of your guests. Better to invite slightly less people than have them crowded around the table, or horror of horrors, without a table at all! Place setting cards are convenient and time saving devices for larger gatherings, but for smaller informal ones this can seem a little controlling. Let everyone choose their own seats, but in case of any reticence or dithering, you could have a mental seating plan in your head just to smooth things along. It can make for more varied conversation if couples and intimate friends are separated slightly to shake things up a bit. As for yourself, you should reserve the seat nearest the kitchen door, so as to create minimum drama when going in and out of the room to serve the meal. Always honour significantly senior or distinguished guests with excellent seats, possibly even at the head of the table.

Lay the table beforehand, with two sets of glasses, one for wine, and one for water. Bring out your finest fabric napkins. In a restaurant the cutlery would perhaps be changed between courses, but for dinner at home, one set is fine. A fresh plate must be provided for each course though, of course. Put out the salt and pepper, and try not to be offended if guests avail themselves of it- everyone's palate is different.

Drinks should be provided generously and liberally, before, during, and after the meal. Pre dinner drinks such as digestifs or maybe even Champagne should be offered upon arrival, and then during the meal there should be suitable wine offered at the table. Make sure refills of drinks are on tap- you could delegate this to another enthusiastic (but not too enthusiastic!) Guest.

When it comes to the actual food, make sure you are serving at the very least two courses, ideally three. It doesnt really seem like a proper dinner party otherwise. Ideally you will have created this lavish feast with your own fair hands, but if you're a disaster in the kitchen then it's perfectly respectable to order it in. Just don't lie about it, that's both cheating, and embarrassing if caught.

Don't keep your guests waiting too long before they eat, remember they will not have eaten beforehand and will probably be drinking, so aim to serve up within forty five minutes of arrival. Some really good artisan bread and butter on the table is always a nice idea, and will fill any gaps in grumbling stomachs if you are running late or even worse, haven't made quite enough food. Aim to serve the main course as soon as possible after the starter. Do offer second helpings if there are any! It's customary to leave a slightly longer gap between the main course and the dessert however, to allow the meal to settle comfortably.

Traditional table protocol dictates that ladies and senior guests should be served first. If hot food is to be served then its polite to encourage people to begin eating as soon as they receive their plate to prevent the meal becoming cold. Heat up plates where appropriate beforehand if you can, to keep food warmer for longer. If serving central dishes on the middle of the table for guests to help themselves, make sure there are enough clean serving spoons on the table.

Try to be thoughtful of your guests preferences, within reason. If someone is only eating the tears of organic non GMO raw unicorns, then that's on them, but most other popular dietary choices are easy to cater for nowadays. Of course, you're not expected to design your entire meal around the single solitary vegan- let the majority rule- but at the very least you could buy in a reheatable option for them, even if it's too complicated to create an entire separate meal from scratch.

After dinner you could finish up with some cheese and biscuits, if you have room, or tea and coffee. Alternatively after dinner drinks or some port. For the languid after dinner lull you could introduce a little after dinner game to keep the conviviality alight, but play this by ear. If everyone is chatting away merrily it's best to leave the party to it's natural devices.

Throwing a Luxury Picnic

Most picnics are informal, no stress, impromptu affairs. However there are occasions such as at Henley or at the races, where the art of the picnic is elevated to a whole other level. At these types of occasions, the eyes of high society will be upon you, and it's worth while as well as being very good fun, to go all out!

The perfect high society picnic should include real cutlery, (no plastic monstrosities here!) Proper napkins, corkscrews and bottle openers, a clean rug to sit on, and a beautiful, preferably wicker hamper to put the food in. If it's a picnic of the fancier kind, consider bringing out the champagne flutes, cool box, and maybe even picnic tables and chairs with starched white linen.

Don't be afraid to enlist the help of guests for contributions, as no one should have to be responsible for the whole show! Split the guests into savoury or sweet duties, and perhaps even ask them in advance what they are bringing to avoid duplication. Poor cooks can always bring drinks...

Traditional games such rounders, cricket, croquet or boules usually go down well at a picnic. These are fun but not too athletic or complicated, so they are accessible for all members of the party.

If the weather's likely to be changeable (here's looking at you UK) then it might be wise to have a second emergency location in your head- perhaps under a pagoda in a park or even someone's conservatory. If it's tipping it down with rain though, please have mercy on your guests and reschedule.

Charming Correspondence

Written communication has changed rapidly in the last decades, and understandably, for reasons of convenience, most people send messages via their phone or the internet rather than putting pen to paper as we used to do. However although handwritten letters are somewhat of an underused art form nowadays, they are unlikely to ever fall completely out of vogue, simply due to the fact that it is lovely, and a nice surprise, to receive things through the post. A lady can easily score social points by sometimes sending real handwritten letters or cards- and the gesture, being less common, is likely to impress and be remembered long after someone else's hastily written instant message or email has been forgotten.

With this in mind, every aspiring lady should cultivate a small writing bureau consisting of fine watermarked A5 writing paper in a white or off white colour and a good quality thickness, such as 100 GSM or higher- and some matching diamond flapped envelopes. In addition, some elegant multipurpose postcard sized notecards for short missives such as thank you notes, and perhaps a small collection of unisex birthday cards for last minute emergencies. The ideal birthday card, of course, is carefully chosen to match the recipient, but a slightly impersonal card is always better than a late card or no card at all. Good quality blue or black ink pens should be used for correspondence- don't use ordinary biros if you can help it, as they make writing look cheap and spindly.

Never send letters written on the computer and printed out. This just looks like boring business communication and lacks personality and finesse.

The highly aspirational could consider availing themselves of some custom made beautifully embossed letter head paper, some hand lined tissue paper envelopes, or perhaps a wax seal with the family Crest. This could be considered overdoing it though...

How to correctly write and address a letter:

- Stick the stamp (ideally 1st class) carefully, not wonkily, in the top right hand corner of the envelope.
- On the actual letter, your own address should be written in the top right hand corner, with the date underneath.
- Begin the letter with "Dear (their name or title),"and end it with "Best wishes, (your name)" or something similar for friends or family. For more formal business letters "Yours sincerely" or "Yours faithfully" should be used. "Kind regards" is a more modern, nebulous invention and is usually better suited to email sign offs. "Regards" is just pure laziness in any situation...or even

sometimes passive aggression in business type situations?
- The P.S or Post Script should only be used for little inconsequential or fun add ons to informal letters. They look unprofessional and disorganised on formal ones.
- Have a mental plan before you begin to write to avoid crossings out, tip ex, and spelling mistakes.
- Save controversial conversations for the phone if you can- remember things that are written down will not be as easily forgotten as angry words spoken. The evidence remains in the physical form of a letter, and even more embarrassingly it can be shown to others.

Types of letters and cards:

Postcards

These are fun to receive but make sure they are light hearted and charming- don't segue into bragging. If you're sending this to people who know each other, try to write something slightly different on each one so as to avoid being repetitive.

Thank you letters/cards

Send these promptly if you can, but remember late is always better than never...

Thank the gift-er effusively and tell them how much you love the gift and why. Little white lies are acceptable here. If you absolutely cannot bring yourself to say that you liked the item in question you could write something vague but appreciative, such as "It was very kind of you to send me a gift for my birthday. Thank you very much!"

If the gift was one of money, then it's classier not to mention the actual sum in your thank you card, or indeed the fact that it was money at all. Say instead "Thank you for your generous gift!"

Try to match the style and effusiveness of your thank you letter with the grandeur of the gift. A hurriedly scribbled missive on a faded cheap note card would be almost insulting if you've been presented with a diamond jewellery set. On the other hand, a long emotional letter on monogrammed notepaper for the tiniest of favours would be slightly ridiculous.

Sympathy cards or letters of condolence

Send these out as quickly as possible after you hear the news. They are very hard to write, so pains must be taken to ensure your missive sounds sincere and warm. When in doubt keep it short and to the point- rambling sentimentality is best received in person- and of course now is not the time to tell them all your news. If you knew the deceased quite well then a little fond anecdote about them is usually appreciated. You could offer to help out, but only do so if you know them well enough and you really mean it.

Christmas cards

If you have a whole squadron of these to send then you're allowed to keep them short, but do make sure they're personal and at least slightly imaginative. "Dear so and so, Happy Christmas, from yours truly" should be the sole preserve of school children. Try to add a short friendly couple of sentences exclusively aimed at them, so that they don't just feel like another tick on a generic Christmas list.

Round Robin's...Whilst understanding that these have arisen from necessity, they really are truly dreadful. An individual sentence or two is all you have to write- maybe phone these people in the new year and catch up personally if you are busy at Christmas and feel like they would like to be updated on all your news.

END

We hope you enjoyed this little guide and feel even better equipped to wow the world as a poised and elegant, fabulous Lady. You GLOW, girl!

Please do visit our new lifestyle website, glowpotion.co.uk for news on our latest publications on etiquette, health, and beauty, and our awesome upcoming beautiful shiny things! Use the code GLOWUP at checkout for a 10% discount on any of our products.

If you enjoyed this book then as a small business we'd really appreciate a review on Amazon. Thank you!

Printed in Great Britain
by Amazon